Lost Profiles

Lost Profiles

MEMOIRS OF CUBISM, DADA, AND SURREALISM

Philippe Soupault

Translated and with a Translator's Note
by Alan Bernheimer

Introduction by Mark Polizzotti

Afterword by Ron Padgett

City Lights Books | San Francisco

Profils perdus was originally published in Paris, France, ©1963 Mercure de France
First City Lights Edition, 2016

Cover art: Le Poète Philippe Soupault, 1922 (oil on canvas),
Robert Delaunay (1885-1941) / Musée National d'Art Moderne

Library of Congress Cataloging-in-Publication Data
Names: Soupault, Philippe, 1897-1990. | Bernheimer, Alan, 1948- translator. |
  Polizzotti, Mark writer of introduction. | Padgett, Ron, 1942- writer of
  afterword.
Title: Lost profiles : memoirs of cubism, dada, and surrealism / Philippe
  Soupault ; translated by Alan Bernheimer ; introduction by Mark Polizzotti
  ; afterword by Ron Padgett.
Other titles: Profils perdus. English | Memoirs of cubism, dada, and
  surrealism
Description: San Francisco : City Lights Publishers, 2016. | Originally
  published in French as Profils perdus by Mercure de France (Paris, 1963).
Identifiers: LCCN 2016020233 | ISBN 9780872867277 (paperback)
Subjects: LCSH: French literature—20th century—History and criticism. |
  Surrealism (Literature)—France—History—20th century. | Dadaist
  literature, French—History—20th century. | Cubism and literature. |
  Authors, French—20th century—Biography. | Authors, French—20th
  century—Anecdotes. | BISAC: BIOGRAPHY & AUTOBIOGRAPHY /
  Literary. |
  BIOGRAPHY & AUTOBIOGRAPHY / Personal Memoirs. | LITERARY
  COLLECTIONS /
  Essays.
Classification: LCC PQ307.S95 S6813 2016 | DDC 840.9/116—dc23
LC record available at https://lccn.loc.gov/2016020233

City Lights books are published at the City Lights Bookstore
261 Columbus Avenue, San Francisco, CA 94133
www.citylights.com

CONTENTS

INTRODUCTION
Philippe Soupault Remembers
by Mark Polizzotti

Philippe Soupault's astute memoir of his literary friendships begins with a visit from four students come to hear his reminiscences of Dada and Surrealism. Like them, I, too, made my youthful pilgrimage to Soupault in search of wisdom from the source. It was 1986, barely four years before his death, and I was just starting work on a biography of André Breton. The idea that this man—one of Surrealism's founding pillars, Breton's co-author on *The Magnetic Fields* in 1919, and a protagonist of the early Dada and Surrealist scandals—might still be alive was startling enough; the fact that he had agreed to see me was mind-boggling.

Soupault was then eighty-eight years old, living in a nondescript residential building near Porte d'Auteuil, at the far end of Paris's sixteenth arrondissement. We talked in the lobby, surrounded by the building's impersonal modern décor, and as I recall we sat at a metal table. I later heard that he was intensely fond of chocolate and kept a huge ball of foil in his apartment, the compressed remnant of many years' worth of wrappers. I remember wishing I had known in time to bring him some.

We spoke, naturally, of Breton—of the two men's meeting via Apollinaire, of the fledgling poet whom Soupault characterized as "timid," of the "authoritarian" Surrealist leader who broke with his old comrade, and of the chastened elder who renewed their friendship after World War II, and who by then seemed "much more interested in astrology" than in literature. We spoke of *The Magnetic Fields*, its genesis and composition, its indebtedness to the psychologist Pierre Janet, and of Breton's neglect of Janet in his own accounts of the book—a purely personal and "spiteful" bias, judged Soupault, "but poets will be poets."

In the end, what Soupault told me was not very different from what he said to his interviewers in "Following in the Footsteps," and no doubt to many others between their visit and mine.[1] But that was hardly the point. This was a voice of living history, relating events it had experienced not in countless academic treatises but first-hand. And more than this, I sensed a generosity, which I expect his young visitors sensed as well; a willingness to share these experiences, and an openness to experience in general, that infused his responses to my questions, as it infuses the pages of *Lost Profiles*.

Readers familiar with the French edition of this memoir will notice that the publishers have reordered the chapters slightly to put Soupault's recollections of Surrealism front and center—appropriately enough. The fact is, if Soupault is remembered today, it is largely because of his ground-floor involvement with a movement that ultimately emerged as one of the most influential of the twentieth century, but that at the time seemed more like youthful hijinks, an as-yet-unfocused response to a dynamite dose of compressed revolt. A contemporary of Breton, Louis Aragon, Paul Eluard, Benjamin Péret, Robert Desnos, and others whose names figure on the original

Surrealist roster, Soupault was one of the "Three Musketeers" (with Breton and Aragon) who founded the seminal avant-garde journal *Littérature* in 1919; co-authored that same year the first book of automatic poetry, *The Magnetic Fields* (and resisted, though not always successfully, Breton's impulse to give the manuscript a stylistic cleanup before it was published); welcomed Tristan Tzara to Paris in 1920 and participated over the next two years in Dada's notorious "demonstrations"; and joined Breton in breaking away from Dada to found their own movement in 1924. In the first *Manifesto*'s honor roll, Breton lists Soupault among the select few who "have performed acts of absolute Surrealism."

For this alone, Soupault would deserve a place in literary history. But those who know him only as a Surrealist poet might be surprised by the range of friendships showcased in *Lost Profiles*, with Proust, Joyce, and Apollinaire, not to mention Blaise Cendrars, Georges Bernanos, René Crevel, and Pierre Reverdy. In this regard, the book could almost act as a personal panorama of twentieth-century modernism, a round-up of the "fantastic individuals" Soupault had the fortune to know in his extraordinary lifetime.

Moreover, Soupault has a talent for encapsulating his subject, whether the young Dadaists ("We were learning arrogance. But it was still only an apprenticeship"), Douanier Rousseau ("Rousseau didn't deign even to respond to those who made fun of him. He knew he was a great painter"), or Reverdy ("Useless to contradict him or even to argue"). There are other lovely glimpses as well, such as Apollinaire in a curio shop ("All this old stuff fascinated him as toys do children"), or Crevel on the telephone, or Cendrars's bedroom-cum-glory hole, or Proust quizzing a café waiter about the precise blossoming habits of the local trees. And he affords precious first-hand insight into the working methods of James Joyce, for Soupault was among those (alongside Samuel Beckett and Eugène Jolas) who helped translate into French the "Anna Livia Plurabelle" passage of *Finnegans Wake*, back when it was still known as *Work in Progress*.

The generosity and open-mindedness I spoke of earlier did not always serve Soupault well. In late 1926, he was among the first to be ousted from the Surrealist ranks for questioning the group's hardline embrace of Soviet Communism—ironic, given his remarks in *Lost Profiles* about the promise of the Russian Revolution. Tarred by his former friends as "counter-revolutionary," he was voted out during a harshly censorious gathering "with all the sanctions that exclusion entails." But behind the political sectarianism lay a second grievance, one perhaps more visceral for Breton: that Soupault, eclectic by nature, was too interested in other currents to pledge his complete fealty to Surrealism. Moreover, his lack of tolerance for the daily café caucus that Breton imposed on members could only work against him. And while we might find his assessment of Surrealism at that point somewhat glib—it "was becoming a literary and pictorial 'school,'" he writes, "a coterie [that] impressed the snobs"—no doubt it also contained enough inconvenient truth to make Breton squirm.

Old grudges die hard, and it's no surprise that *Lost Profiles* did not find much favor among the latter-day Surrealists when it was published in 1963. The reasons are easy to guess: Soupault had been dishonorably discharged from the movement many years before, and his memoir includes some less than flattering portrayals of his former comrades-in-arms—in addition to ascribing more importance to Dada, and less to Surrealism's own posterity, than Surrealism's remaining members would have liked.

To be fair, there are some grounds on which the Surrealist firebrands had a point. Soupault tends to assign himself the starring role a bit more than is warranted, and he sometimes muddles his chronology. To cite two examples: The broadside against Anatole France, *A Corpse*, was issued not under Dada, as he says, but in 1924, well after Dada had imploded, and the scandal it provoked was linked with the birth of Surrealism (while the much less successful "trial" of Maurice Barrès, which Soupault presents as a direct consequence of *A Corpse*, actually took place three years earlier and helped hasten Dada's end). No doubt more important, Soupault suggests that *The Magnetic Fields* was composed as a result of Dada's demise, whereas the book was written the year before Paris Dada began, and more properly constitutes a first stab at the kinds of preoccupations that would characterize early Surrealism five years later. As strict history, the reader is advised to take some of this memoir with the proverbial grain of salt.

But again, that's hardly the point, is it? What Soupault offers is not the exact furniture placement—there are plenty of tomes for that—but the taste, feel, and smell of a literary environment, as he lived it and as he evocatively and affectionately conveys it. *Lost Profiles* will not supplant Richard Ellmann's biography of Joyce, for instance, or Michel Sanouillet's magisterial history of Paris Dada. What it does do is flesh out the human story, provide the personal underpinnings and anecdotal contour on which such monumental studies are built, and that make them worth reading. It also invites us to share in the unique perspective of a man who, by thinking outside the norms of his time and place, wound up on the inside for some of the most thrilling moments of our modern intellectual history.

—March 2016

Translator's Note

An anecdote about Henri Rousseau, le Douanier, recounted in Roger Shattuck's *The Banquet Years*, first alerted and attracted me to Philippe Soupault's 1963 memoir, *Profils perdus*, and so the first in this line of thanks goes to Shattuck and the sumptuous meal he makes of the roots of the avant-garde in France. Next, to Ron Padgett, who nearly 50 years ago awoke me to the idea of translating for pleasure, and whose own recent translation of Guillaume Apollinaire's *Zone: Selected Poems* continues to inform and inspire. Padgett's account, in the afterword to the present volume, of meeting the older Soupault in Paris in the mid-1970s, turning the profiling mirror back on the author, is only the most obvious instance of his generosity and encouragement in this project.

My translation itself is indebted to several advisors who helped me through some rough passages, especially Leah Brumer, but also Mark Polizzotti, Stephen Emerson, and Bill Graves. I am grateful to Timothy Young of the Beinecke Library, Betsy Jolas, and Christine Chemetoff Soupault for generous help with photographs.

The chapters about Pierre Reverdy and René Crevel first appeared in *Catamaran Literary Reader*, thanks to editors Catherine Segurson and Thomas Christensen. Tom also advised me on finding a publisher, as did Kit Schluter, and finally Brent Cunningham, who paved the way to City Lights, where Garrett Caples and Elaine Katzenberger welcomed and supported my effort to bring Philippe Soupault to a wider English-speaking audience and help commemorate the centenary of what he calls the jolt that Dada and then Surrealism produced.

—*Alan Bernheimer*

Lost Profiles

Following in the Footsteps

FOUR YOUNG PEOPLE, STUDENTS, come to visit with the pretext of bringing me some poems. They look at me so closely that I get the impression of being some strange creature in their eyes. They observe my gestures and looks and they listen to what I tell them without interrupting. I am a little irritated at being the object of this examination. I suddenly remember that, at their age, accompanied by my friends Louis Aragon and André Breton, I would (leaving all modesty aside) pay visits to Apollinaire or Paul Valéry, but I was less watchful.

Finally, the ice is broken. The least timid of the four students begins to ask me questions. What especially interests them is less what I currently think than what I thought when I was their age. What they would like to know is why and how the Dada movement was born. But for them it is already ancient history. They even seem to forget that for the generations preceding theirs, Dada is synonymous with scandal. I try to explain to them:

"It's because of the scandal it provoked that the Dada movement was misunderstood and mischaracterized. Along with my Dadaist friends, I believed, and I still believe, that it was necessary to cause scandal, even that it was one of the essential raisons d'être of this 'movement.' I am convinced, and the future proved me right, that my contemporaries were wrong to consider the Dada movement a schoolboy prank, a student protest, and a publicity campaign launched by upstart scribblers to call attention to their writing. It was much more than this, and today I am tempted to attach much more importance to it than when I was one of those responsible."

In reality, I think the movement was the most violent and spectacular demonstration of a whole generation in revolt.

"Poetic revolt," one of the young students reminds me.

"Without a doubt. The prophets of this movement were poets and, above all, Arthur Rimbaud. It is the poet of *Illuminations* who proposed and foretold the revolt. He created, for many who were young in 1914, a climate favorable to a liberation. But those who were the leading thinkers of the so-called Belle Epoque, Rimbaud's contemporaries, did not understand, didn't even listen to this warning. They were already out of tune with their time, with the youth of their day."

I feel the need to recall for my interlocutors the names of those who were considered the representatives of French thought before and during World War I. Anatole France, considered a tremendous genius; Paul Bourget, who played the role of literary dictator; René Bazin, the herald of the "right-minded"; Maurice Barrès, the anarchist converted to chauvinism. When I cite these names, the students smile, but they laugh out loud when I declare to them that the famous poets of this period were Jean Aicard, Edmond Rostand, and Jean Richepin, whereas Stéphane Mallarmé and the Symbolists were viewed as ridiculous and harmless amateurs.

"We read a lot, and we did not agree either with our elders or with the 'masters' whose reputation and success were imposed on us. Very young, I was sixteen, after my first baccalaureate exam, I had the somewhat vague but persistent

*Philippe Soupault, late
1980s, Ré Soupault*

impression that I was witnessing the end of a world, the decline
of a civilization. Rimbaud, he who had fled this world, seemed
to me the only guide. But my high school comrades and I were
not expecting what was to come. We were, truth to tell, like the
bourgeois and petit-bourgeois milieu in which we lived, very
poorly informed."

At the end of our adolescence, the war "broke out." I
think it is very hard now, in the overwhelming light of the
Second World War, to understand what the First World War
represented for us adolescents.

If I can take a short cut, by way of example: ten years later
one of my best friends, a high school comrade, a very talented
designer and son of a Paris attorney, took his own life in New
York. "One cannot live in a world where everyone cheats," he
wrote me to explain his act of despair. He summed up in one
sentence the feeling of a greater number of young people than
you might have thought.

Since I was interested in literature, I had to realize that the famous literary people (save for rare exceptions like Romain Rolland[2], who was considered a traitor and whose articles we thus could not read) accepted and even exalted the tragic misunderstandings that were the cause and consequence of the First World War. If one rereads the "literary" output of this period and what was called propaganda, it is astounding that this "literature" (which was already outraging a great number of combatants) could be appreciated so widely and for so long by those in the rear who boasted of belonging to a nation which they claimed was endowed with the sharpest critical mind.

At the time of the armistice, I thought, and I wasn't alone, that all writers were permanently discredited. I was wrong. After this four-year war that, for all who returned from it, evoked a tragedy "filled with blood and fury" and also with mud, those who were ironically called patriotic writers certainly intended to continue imposing their dictatorship and exercising their influence. Many young writers from before the war (Alain Fournier, Charles Péguy, to cite just two examples) had been killed. We spoke rather cynically of the lost generation.

But among the survivors at the end of the war was a poet that I wanted to meet, because I had read his poems and had sent him those I was beginning to write and publish, a poet who seemed to me to be the only one who was claiming the discovery of a new world, who more or less deliberately rejected the conformism of the official masters of literature and art, since the same conformism reigned in the domain of the arts, painting, or music. His name was Guillaume Apollinaire. Despite the goodwill gestures that he had unfortunately made to what I considered an intolerable dictatorship, this authentic poet continued to be the laughingstock of pundits and journalists because he spoke of the new spirit and the future. I was astonished that he could stand provoking scandals, almost in spite of himself, by publishing poems without punctuation and warmly defending the Cubist painters. I already envied him for causing scandal and being abused by those I considered hypocritical adversaries. It was at this time that I began to realize the importance of scandal. Certain reservations notwithstanding, I was captivated by the personality of Apollinaire, who, I told myself, remembering a word of Rimbaud's, was a visionary. He helped confirm my point of view and encourage in me the spirit of rebellion whose fierceness I did not yet appreciate.

Remember too that at this time we witnessed, without being well informed, an upheaval that unleashed a campaign of slander, of false reports—the Russian Revolution. Russia was for me the country of Gogol, Tolstoy, Chekhov, and Dostoevsky. For my generation, the word revolution, lit by historical memories, held an incomparable prestige. I believed that our entire civilization was going to be called into question, that the Russian Revolution was the start of a new era, that the whole world was going to be transformed, that it was a global revolution starting in Moscow, as a revolution had started in 1789 in the place de la Bastille.

I was still naïve, and all the same less naïve than my fellow citizens who were furious, especially the bourgeois that I lived among who worried about the collapse of "Russian values" and were terribly uneasy about what was called Bolshevism.

It was in this climate that I met two young medical students dressed in sky-blue uniforms. First, André Breton, whom Guillaume Apollinaire introduced me to, then Louis Aragon. Camaraderie first, then friendship, sharing experiences, enthusiasms, and especially indignation. The rediscovery of these feelings was all the more precious to me since my friend from childhood, my best friend, had just been killed at the front.

We were, the three of us, like explorers leaving to discover the world of literature, but explorers who were severely appraising the fauna of arts and letters. We were prepared to be pitiless.

Thanks to Theodore Fraenkel, another medical student friend of Louis Aragon and André Breton, we were captivated and influenced by the devastating humor of Alfred Jarry.

The four students, who were listening attentively to this account until now (they were used to taking lessons), couldn't help giggling. I resumed:

Although we knew where we stood and that the youth of our generation had lost its sense of deference and hierarchy during the war, we were still impressed by certain writers and painters. Apollinaire had just died and we were saddened by his death; even more, we had the feeling that we were being thwarted, that a new gap had been opened between our generation and the one that had survived. We were trying to make choices. We were going to look closely at Paul Valéry, more and more disappointing as he cleverly cultivated success (he was already thinking about the Académie française and royalties); at André Gide, whom we were curious to know better because he had proposed in his *Caves du vatican* the character of Lafcadio, who captivated us because we believed we were somewhat like him; at Paul Claudel, whom we were the first to hail as a great poet but who rejected us roughly and stupidly, as was his custom.

The poet Pierre Reverdy, who published our poems in his *Nord-Sud* review, fascinated us because, like us, for the time being, he was interested only in poetry, which at this time seemed to us the only acceptable language, the sole means of making contact with the world. We had, however, some doubts. The literary world and that of the poets (Max Jacob, Francis Carco, Blaise Cendrars, André Salmon) appeared to us suspiciously tepid and, above all, shapeless. Rebellion was fermenting.

We shared our anger. It was at this point that we picked up some signals as startling as if they came from another planet. But first we wanted to assert our independence by publishing a magazine which we, who were already stupidly called the Three Musketeers, would edit. We hesitated a long time before choosing a name. In our naiveté, we thought about calling it *Le monde nouveau*[3] or *Le nouveau monde* (quite a task), but we were uncertain enough to consult Paul Valéry, who ironically and speciously persuaded us (we didn't at first understand the irony) to adopt the title *Littérature* (underlined, he said, and by antiphrasis recalling Verlaine's ironical line, "Tout le reste est littérature" [All the rest is literature.]).

Why did this 24-page, small-format magazine, whose very eclectic table of contents gathered the writers we judged the least conformist at this time, see such success from its first issue? I must record it as a symptom but I can't explain it, especially remembering that Marcel Proust, who was not a contributor, wrote me a twelve-page letter to subscribe and congratulated us on our audacity. Perhaps this publication, while positioned timidly enough, made it possible to foresee the "*orages désirés*."[4]

Thanks to *Littérature,* contacts were established with those who, like us, refused to accept the taboos that the patriotic writers, in declaring victory, wanted to impose on us.

The end of the war did not, indeed, represent victory to us but rather a sudden awakening. And so we welcomed the overtures of a group of young people from Zurich, Romanian and German émigrés, who published a magazine and organized events in a little theater called, much to our displeasure, the Cabaret Voltaire (always the classics!).

All the same, we realized our kinship quickly enough. We received provocative letters from a certain Tristan Tzara asking us to collaborate in his publications and participate in a movement that he claimed was revolutionary and that he had baptized the Dada movement, choosing at random from the dictionary a name that meant nothing and committed to nothing. This young Romanian who had emigrated to Switzerland was the most perceptive and the most energetic of all the young people who were starting (it was only the beginning) to anticipate and to hope for, meanwhile working together to bring about, the reign of the absurd (a reign that is not yet over).

This thought meets with approval by my young friends, which doesn't surprise me. I know they know what the fascination and prestige of the absurd means for several generations. They know it much better than we knew it.

Not only did Tristan Tzara present performances in Zurich that unfortunately recalled those of the Belle Époque in Montmartre cabarets, he also tried to make contact with people who seemed to him ripe for the intellectual revolt that he foresaw. He succeeded in making common cause with the Paris poets, the founders of *Littérature*, with the German painters and writers (Max Ernst, Hugo Ball, Kurt Schwitters), more anarchists at that time than creative artists, as well as with two French painters (Marcel Duchamp, Francis Picabia) who had emigrated to New York and one of their friends, the American painter and photographer Man Ray, the three of whom relished the art of making scandal and published the magazine *391*.[5]

So far, this was only the initial groundwork. The Dada movement did not reach its full significance and explosive force until Tristan Tzara came to Paris to meet those who, with Louis Aragon, André Breton, and myself, were becoming aware of our desire to be done with the literature of the past, with all its sacrosanct traditions. We repeated as a slogan this line of Apollinaire's, "À la fin tu es las de ce monde ancien." [In the end you are tired of this old world.] I must acknowledge that at that time we knew what we no longer wanted but did not yet know where we wanted to go. We especially longed to destroy, despite a certain timidity that we suffered from and which was called, astonishingly, our "good upbringing." "How well mannered they are," said the Countess of Noailles, a remark that infuriated us. They'd see! The arrival of Tristan Tzara, which I compared to a bomb, was the starting point and the opportunity for the rebellion.

What must be remembered, what remains for me one of the important points in this history, is that at the very beginning we formed a team; I mean we exerted a decisive influence on one another at the same time that we rejected outside pressure with equal force and intransigence, dismissing caution warnings from our elders. We were learning arrogance. But it was still only an apprenticeship. Tzara, more experienced and less hampered than we by friendships and memories, proposed that we organize some public performances. The first of the events took place in the rue aux Ours in a neighborhood chosen because it was not "snobbish." The poets recited their poems, and the painters showed their paintings to an attentive crowd, bigger than we could have expected.

Everything went along very calmly but, at the end of the performance, Tristan Tzara succeeded in causing a genuine scandal by proposing to compose a poem on the spot, in front of the audience, picking words written on scraps of paper thrown into a hat that he withdrew at random. This was too much. People hissed. And the event ended in great disarray. Although slightly concerned, we were delighted with this outcome, because it was this initial scandal that impressed upon us that if we wanted to articulate and spread our rebellion, we had to systematically cause scandal.

Tristan Tzara, outstanding impresario, persuaded us to organize other performances, first at the Salon des Indépendants, where the thirteen Dada manifestoes were read that expressed the violence of the rebellion of those who were ironically called (all the press spoke angrily about us) the Dadaists.

At the same time that we understood the necessity for scandal (because it seemed to us, not unreasonably, that since the armistice, people, notably former combatants as well as intellectuals, were trying to forget, to resume the best possible little life, and were settling into indifference and even—it was a bit the case with us—skepticism), we were getting a taste for it. I think success would have intoxicated us less than the indignation and wrath of our contemporaries. The insults that were abundantly hurled at us in every tone, not to mention the rotten eggs, tomatoes, and pieces of meat, persuaded us that we were on the right path. So we didn't hesitate to collaborate very actively with Tzara to repeat our experiments with public performances, first at the Théâtre de l'Oeuvre and then at the Salle Gaveau. In crowded and rowdy halls, we tried to outdo our arrogance and tossed challenges to all who claimed to assert their privilege in defending what they called tradition. With what pleasure we organized shooting galleries! We were determined to spare no one, not even those we had at first admired and respected. And of course, within our own team, no one-upmanship was avoided. No more limits. We were truly wild. What seems to me in hindsight to be a powerful symptom was the enormous repercussion that, despite our increasing insolence, surprised even us. We didn't clearly understand why these performances, which were deliberately more and more scandalous and in which the absurd was conscientiously glorified, provoked such a strong backlash in the press and the public. On reflection, I think these unusual performances, these incessant provocations and the violent invectives that we published in numerous magazines and publications and in open letters that some daily papers printed (with insulting comments) were interpreted quite rightly as the onset of a moral revolution that could become dangerous. Paraphrasing a famous statement, one journalist who didn't spare platitudes wrote, "It is more than a riot, it's a revolution." Deeply indignant, but also worried (which continued to delight and encourage us), journalists, critics, and writers began to understand that the Dada movement was much more than a student prank. The most perceptive and attentive critic of the time, Jacques Rivière, the editor of the *Nouvelle revue française*, a magazine that in 1922 enjoyed immense prestige and exercised considerable influence, was the first to seriously study in depth what was beginning to be called the Dada phenomenon. He published a long study, a very long article titled "Reconnaissance à Dada" [Gratitude to Dada], in which he explained the range and consequence of this movement. He maintained that Dada was going to try— not without some chance of success—to destroy all the established values, the literary practices, and the moral bias that the great captains of literature and journalism wanted to continue imposing, blinded by the victory of armies and the partisans of the various traditional formalisms.

Thanks to these violent reactions, we were confirmed in our intention to make a clean sweep. More than ever, it was a matter for us of denying and disowning. A phrase that had been proposed by Tristan Tzara served by way of a motto: "The absence of system is still a system, but it is still better."

All of us, presidents of the Dada movement because we had decided that all the participants were presidents, were becoming great friends. We recruited new comrades, such as the poet, painter, and musician Georges Ribemont-Dessaignes and the dandy Jacques Rigaut. We met up every day at a café, most often in Montparnasse, in all its glory at that time. Our evenings stretched until dawn. We were not looked on favorably, since we occasionally touched off or participated in brawls. One of the most famous of these evenings, a banquet given in honor of the poet Saint-Pol Roux at the Closerie de Lilas, left a noisy memory in the history of Montparnasse. I was even accused of swinging from a chandelier to sweep the plates and glasses off the table. The scandal was more serious even than for the earlier events, because this time we had not presented a performance but had directly attacked the literati, the artists, the institutions, and the politics of the rulers of France and Europe. The press decided to boycott us and no longer mention us. But never was so much spoken and written about Dada.

More and more young poets and writers sympathized with us and asked to participate in our meetings, notably René Crevel, Robert Desnos, Jacques Prévert, Jacques Baron. Too rapidly for my liking, Dadaism, as the movement was called from that point on, adopted the customs of a congregation, which was contrary to its spirit. It was likewise at this time that several painters who had been among the first Dadaists—Arp, Max Ernst, André Masson, Man Ray—made their influence felt. In the plastic arts it was more difficult to disown, and perhaps only Francis Picabia succeeded in giving his work the quality of absolute revolt, of anti-painting. But despite errors in interpretation, Dada exerted a profound influence whose depth the Dadaists themselves overlooked. All the taboos that had been blindly respected for a half century were seen to rapidly disintegrate. The best example was the confrontation we undertook on the day that Anatole France died. When the Academician, who was considered not only the best French writer but also (this made us smile) a thinker and moralist of extreme subtlety—assured of immortality as the most untouchable of idols—died, the Dadaists published a pamphlet entitled *Un cadavre* [A Corpse] on the eve of his state funeral, in which we expressed with fierce insolence our scorn for the character and the work of a man the world passionately admired and respected.

The disapproval and indignation surpassed our hopes. I had the impression, nevertheless, that we had "struck a nerve" and that, basically, hypocrisy aside, people didn't disagree with us. Our taking a stance, which still seemed rather courageous, resulted in Dada's being taken seriously.

This, which we considered a more significant success than our performances, prompted us to hold a public trial of Maurice Barrès, still at the height of his fame. As a result of this "trial," which was, moreover, quite pitiful and poorly staged, Barrès was "condemned to die." When he heard of this sentence, I know that the writer, who fifty years before had wanted to be the "prince of youth," was rather flattered that young people were still interested in him. But he absolutely did not understand that what he took for a joke had deeper consequences for his fame than the letters from readers he received following the articles he spearheaded in the *Echo de Paris*.

This trial of Maurice Barrès marked for my friends and me the onset of Dada's death pangs. Tzara and I still hoped that we could continue to carry out activity, but several of our friends, especially Breton, no longer thought so. Rivalries among groups, struggles for influence, and various ambitions broke up the team. I was the first to declare this "break-up."

My four listeners interrupted me. They wanted to know how Dada died.

I'm trying to remember. It was rather sad: the death throes of friendships. First, one can't continuously repudiate without wanting to repudiate oneself. We all had the impression, at the moment when Dada's influence and importance was growing, even while greater and greater numbers of young poets were joining up, that we were at a standstill, that henceforth we could only repeat ourselves. And that seemed to us to already look like old age, like driveling on, that we were ourselves on the point of proposing an aesthetic and a morality. One last event, the visit to the Church of Saint-Julien-le-Pauvre, was a failure. An exhibit at the Galerie Montaigne was only half successful. And however individually we had become, without false modesty, notorious, we were considered future great writers. We did not enjoy this irony and it made us mad. I remember my anger and Louis Aragon's when we had this sentence in *Le temps* from the pen of Paul Souday, who was then the most influential critic: "When M. Louis Aragon and M. Philippe Soupault present themselves to the Académie française in some thirty years, they will be a bit embarrassed if a competitor unearths these sorry flights of fancy." We were already being buried. Nevertheless, we were too young, younger even than our age, not to soon recover from the death of Dada. One more demolition, after all. What was sadder and rather demoralizing to me, was to witness the often bitter quarrels, the arguments, among my comrades in arms, whose friendship I refused to forget.

The systematic demolition scheme that had been Dada had not, for that matter, absorbed all our activity. There existed a realm where we had never stopped feeling like ourselves, where we could breathe freely—that of poetry. During these years of conflict, the great mediator remained Arthur Rimbaud. We had also rediscovered Lautréamont. The destinies of these two poets seemed to me to justify what I still thought was my vocation, poetry, which assured us liberty. The vocation that I continue to deem the highest. André Breton and

I, in the course of daily conversations, had discussed poetry at length, explored this realm, analyzed works of poetry, *Illuminations* and *Les chants de Maldoror*, various texts by Apollinaire, and the poetry of Pierre Reverdy. It seemed to us that poetry was still paralyzed by a number of taboos and that it was not fulfilling the possibilities of the dream, which André Breton had studied and whose powers and privileges he revealed to me while introducing me to the works of Freud. We had a kind of revelation.

We were struck by the remarkable importance of images and compared those that ornamented everyday language, those that poets worthy of the name had created, with those that illuminated dreams. Excited by this revelation, I thought only of pursuing experiments, and, as in many other areas, I have preserved this attitude while regretting having perhaps remained alone in preserving it, fearing, since the death of Dada—which marked me deeply—dogmatism, systems, and definitions. I was against all bias, all preconceptions. At this time, while André Breton and I had not yet been baptized Surrealists, we wanted foremost to devote ourselves only to experiments. They led us to regard poetry as a liberation, as the possibility (perhaps the sole one) to give the mind a freedom that we had known only in our dreams and to free us from the entire machinery of logic.

In the course of our research we had noticed, indeed, that, freed from all critical pressure and scholarly habit, the mind provided images and not logical propositions, and that if we were willing to adopt what the psychiatrist Pierre Janet called automatic writing, we would record texts in which we described a "universe" heretofore unexplored. So we decided to give ourselves two weeks to write collaboratively a work in which we prohibited correcting or erasing our "flights of fancy."

We had no trouble respecting this deadline, and with growing delight we became acquainted with texts that we decided to publish under the title *Les champs magnétiques*. What we at first cautiously called a method was born from this book, which we baptized Surrealism in memory of Guillaume Apollinaire, who had characterized as Surrealist one of his texts, *Onirocritique*. We were in raptures, André Breton and I. We communicated our enthusiasm to Louis Aragon, the first to understand straightaway the importance, the scope, and the future of our discovery and who wrote with his amazing virtuosity *Une vague des rêves* [A Wave of Dreams], the second Surrealist text, which proved to us the excellence of our "method."

And soon, our other friends, Éluard (not without hesitation), Desnos, Péret, and Crevel, were won over. We were certain we had liberated poetry. After so many years, I maintain this conviction, but I think that having participated so actively in the Dada movement greatly helped to free us and allowed us to carry out the experiment that was the birth of Surrealism.

We wanted to win over in other fields and we suggested that our painter friends, Max Ernst in particular, try the same experiment. Which he did, with enthusiasm and conviction. His successes were dazzling. André Masson also was interested at first in Surrealism, taking the measure of its power and all that it could bring to painting by liberating it. Picasso himself, although customarily on guard, was not unappreciative. In my opinion, Surrealism brought about the end of Cubism. In the musical realm, which was colonized by snobs, Surrealism wasn't able to exercise any influence, which explains the decadence in the French school of music up until Messaien. We tried, André Breton and I, to transpose our Surrealist experiments to the stage, and we wrote two plays, but (rapidly persuaded by the commercialization of French theater) we quickly abandoned these experiments, which were taken up with great success twenty years later by Eugene Ionesco. As for film, where we had tried to point out some new directions, the influence of Surrealism was very distinctly felt, but only belatedly.

I hoped that Breton and I, supported by our friends and by the enthusiastic young poets, would be able to pursue our experiments, our explorations. I was thinking only about poetry. I was wrong. André Breton wanted to systematize (which was his vocation, as I found out only too late) Surrealism, to impose rules and directives. Thanks to the fervent friendship I felt for him, I did not rebel (not yet). Besides, the love of a woman and of revolt for revolt's sake (Rimbaud's example) diverted me from my friendships. I did not dream of exploiting the undeniable and growing success of Surrealism. After six years of complete fidelity, I could no longer bear the atmosphere of the little coterie where we extolled each other, an atmosphere that seemed harder and harder to breathe. I had no ambition because I had too much pride. When my friends made the mistake of wanting to put Surrealism in the service of a political party, I broke away from their group, not without sadness but without bitterness. I wanted to get away from it. I wanted to get to know the world and escape from literary circles, aesthetic or political. Without regret, I left for some lengthy travels. Surrealism, guided by André Breton and Paul Éluard, was transformed. Artaud, who had been one of the effective experimenters since the beginning of Surrealism, as well as Roger Vitrac and Robert Desnos, violently denounced the new direction of what in their eyes was becoming a literary and pictorial "school," a coterie, a tribunal—everything that I too wished to avoid. Surrealism, despite my defection and that of its most vigorous adherents, and thanks especially to the will and perseverance of André Breton and his new friends, extended its influence, impressed the snobs. It was a new experiment, but in a very different spirit from what I wished.

New adherents appeared, of whom the most restless were three Spaniards—Buñuel, a director who was the most genuine Surrealist in the realm of film, and two painters, Miró and Salvador Dalí, the latter wavering still between the careers of clown, painter, and businessman. These three "artists" exploited more than they served Surrealism, despite their acrobatic virtuosity. My estrangement notwithstanding, I realized that Surrealism, such as I had dreamed it, was losing all its purity for me.

But, despite its popularization, which was visible and continues to be visible in posters, shop windows, and vocabulary, Surrealism has never ceased exercising its power. I cannot forget that, in spite of the excommunications that always seemed ridiculous to me, like all excommunications, I have never ceased to be Surrealist. Indeed, Surrealism is not a literary school or a religion. It is the expression of an attitude and a state of mind and especially the expression of freedom. All the rules, all the definitions, all the masks imposed on it have not diminished its power. Historically, one can claim that it is lost in the sands, but like a river, it continues to bore its course deep underground. Surrealism, like Dadaism, has become an "epoch" in the history of the human spirit, and it is not for me, as witness and participant, to judge its significance. I think, however, that after a quarter of a century it remains very great. What seems singular and difficult to explain (I turn then to my visitors) is that after the Second World War it is only in England, with its "angry young men," that one was able to witness a jolt comparable to what Dadaism and then Surrealism produced.

And this time, it was I that put the question. My interviewers replied with only these words: "For us, that's another story. . . ."

Guillaume Apollinaire

FOR FORTY YEARS SINCE his death, the glory of Guillaume Apollinaire, the glory he so desired, has exalted but distorted his memory. His complete works (or nearly), his private papers, and numerous studies devoted to his work and influence have been published. He has become a "great poet." Those who knew him are amazed that a statue, in a sense, has been erected of someone who was the opposite of a statue. In fact, Guillaume Apollinaire was a man whose contours were hard to define. It's questionable whether he himself even knew his true dimensions. When you looked at him or talked with him, you always wondered who you were dealing with, and vice versa. He had a conspiratorial smile. It seemed easy, at least, to understand his tastes: he loved to eat and make love, was in love with literature (good or bad, ancient or modern) and good painting, adored curios and knickknacks, anecdotes and gossip, and rare books—especially racy ones. But it was harder, for me anyway, to know what he wanted or where he wanted to go. He was both audacious and timid, a conformist hungry for official praise but a prankster, pedantic and ironic, curious and lazy, irritable and indifferent. He displayed a tolerance and indulgence that was unpardonable to the young man of seventeen I was when I knew him. He loved to mix with the weirdest people, who reeked—to put it mildly—of mold and decay. It's probably still too soon for me to name names. But it must be said that this "liberality" played him false. He would have liked to be popular, and nothing thwarts that more than slander and malicious gossip. Yet he was never afraid to shock or astonish and sometimes, more rarely, to cause a scandal.

It's no doubt because I suffered from what his enemies (despite himself, he had many) malevolently and unfairly called his duplicity that I can't forget that he was vexing. I suppose he wanted to build a legend around himself. To an extent, he certainly succeeded. But certainly not in the way he intended.

Because even if he is now bedecked with tributes and praise, we forget that he was first of all an audacious poet, the most audacious of his time, and next that it's to him that all the most celebrated painters of our time owe their fame. Thanks to the publication of some regrettable verse discovered in linen closets belonging to passing objects of his affection and perhaps his love, many of our contemporaries imagine that Guillaume Apollinaire was a prolific, facile, and elegiac poet. When it came to poetry, especially his own—and not love poems—Apollinaire proved himself to be extremely scrupulous, scrupulous to the point of hesitancy. Many of his poems, even some that could have been considered among his best, were thrown into the wastebasket. But, since he loved experiments, he did his best to recover the same tone and the same language a little later. And he sought to acknowledge in other poets a similar care not to be satisfied with repeating themselves.

I can't forget that it was he who first gave me the confidence and permission to be a poet—and I believed him. It's also to his credit that all those who saw and heard him can still look at each other without hatred.

I often walked beside the "flâneur des deux rives."[6] Because

Guillaume Apollinaire, 1902

I owe him so much, I can't recall without emotion a gray winter morning in 1917 when I bought an issue of the *Nord-Sud* review that Pierre Reverdy edited and read these few lines:

> *Your tongue*
> *the goldfish in the bowl*
> *of your voice*

A poem by Apollinaire (was it good? I didn't permit myself to judge) always caused a stir but, in me, enthusiasm and joy. Guillaume Apollinaire did not want to lead a school of poetry (he told me so). He was instead what he himself called a signal rocket. He invoked the heavens and called the stars like familiar birds. He loved to surround himself with looks, gestures, and words. He needed friends. But yet he could be haughty, even fierce. The end of the First World War was one of those times when you had to "arrive," when success couldn't wait. He and others strove to make themselves heard at almost any cost. But poetry came first for him. He was proud of being a poet, and reveled in the legend that was already settling around him, bit by bit, like snow. He could be joyful, and he always smiled with pleasure in saying how well his friends wrote. He loved them too much, and I often heard him, who had such good taste, lose perspective when he praised the work of his friends, painters, writers, journalists. But his confidence wasn't always so strong. He was terrified by the memory of prison and of those who had betrayed him then.[7] You would have thought he was wary of ghosts. He feared the past and especially his own past, of which he never spoke. What interested him, and interested me, was the future. For me, the real Apollinaire was the one who wrote:

> *Let's go, for God's sake*
> *Let's go*

But maybe he didn't share my view. I should have suspected as much. He did not forget old "things." I can't help recalling that, when he was working at the censor's office in 1917, which was then located in the Bourse, where he would go to meet his old friend André Billy, we'd often walk down the rue de la Banque, one of the saddest streets in Paris. Near one of the municipal buildings there was a secondhand-dealer's stand. Apollinaire would stay for an hour (no doubt time moved very slowly for me), looking over every little item on display: old keys, chipped plates, napkin rings, pen holders, rusty razors (I had plenty of time to check). All this old stuff fascinated him as toys do children. He never bought a thing. Even so, the dealer wouldn't get mad. Apollinaire would ask, "How much is this?" and then carefully replace his find without even waiting for the answer. "It's not worth anything," he'd confide to me. But he'd pick it up and inspect it again. I thought he wanted to be rid of me, that it was a polite way of getting me to say good-bye and leave. But he would take hold of my sleeve and ask me to stay.

Sometimes I would go visit him at home. At the end of his life he lived in an apartment on the top floor of a building at the corner of the boulevard Saint-Germain and the rue Saint-Guillaume. Tiny rooms and narrow halls. His room (the one where he died) was adorned with paintings by his friends, Picasso, Braque, Marie Laurencin. His "office" was lit by a fanlight and also served as his dining room. He felt very much at home there.

If I describe this decor, it is to help me remember the choices that reflected his somewhat middle-class tastes, his love of collecting, his satisfaction in having his own place, and his need for comfort, modest as it was.

I was astonished at the setting that this, to me, great poet had more or less spontaneously created. With my own eyes, I saw him write many poems there, particularly "Ombre." It was an unforgettable sight. I also watched him correcting proofs. He took tremendous pains, but it didn't keep him from smiling and even bursting into laughter. I admired and envied his terrific nonchalance.

I continue to believe that Apollinaire's poetry, that is to say *Alcools* and *Calligrammes*, has a richness and a boldness that are truly exceptional, especially if you remember the period when it was conceived. This inspired poet sought, without always succeeding, but in very good faith, "something new," as he called it. What he most valued, when it came to poetry, was novelty, in every sense of the word. His cherished ghosts, especially Heine's and sometimes Ronsard's, haunted his dreams and dictated certain turns of phrase, but most of the time [*la plupart du temps*] (one of his favorite expressions) he deliberately sought the unknown. No doubt his erudition (contrived or genuine, no one can judge) often got in his way. But it's no less true that it was he who gave the young poets of his time the permission "to go faster and farther," as he had so ardently desired and demanded.

It is above all because of this gift that my, that our, debt, to him is immense and that it behooves us, forty years after his death, not to forget it despite the temptation to do so.

The painters, for their part, even with the best intentions, shouldn't underestimate the phenomenal confidence he granted and inspired in them. He allowed them not to abandon what was most alive in themselves, most powerful, most intense. And especially, he exalted what he called, inappropriately enough, "the new spirit," an expression vague enough to satisfy artists and intrigue art lovers, but that authorized both the best and the worst painters to give free rein to their instincts, to leave behind all academisms.

He prided himself on being a poet and prophet. He easily adopted the tone of someone who predicts the future, more in writing than in speech. He wasn't so wrong. For those who listened to him at the end of his life, when he was most sure of himself, he always seemed a quarter century ahead of his friends and acquaintances.

He was indisputably extraordinary, and that's why it is a shame that some try to distort his character and reduce him to the rank of "great man" for timid people.

Ode to Guillaume Apollinaire

Poor Guillaume my friend
they cover you with glory with flowers with ashes
great man in quotes statue in bronze
with the patina of fame
they overwhelm you with everything you so disliked
they crown your skull with laurels
they rattle your skeleton to strike sparks

Dear Guillaume my friend
I haven't forgotten your smile
nor your quiet sniggers
nor the dread of oblivion and of ingratitude
there you are, finally bedecked
crowned phantom phantom
what more can they give you
that you so disliked
glory honor medals
and then love into the bargain
the love of idiots and imbeciles
and of these girls
who don't know how to see
past the end of your nose

Remember the sunrise
at daybreak out in Auteuil
and thirst without a cent for drink
the bazaar that you ransacked
desperately and exhaustively
without knowing what you sought
to load your life a little more
with old plates old books
and the sunlight in rock crystal.

I knew Guy at the gallop
when he was a soldier
and it was sad very sad
like a day without bread or moon
and he was prouder than Artaban
because he was a second lieutenant
in the infantry at war
jealous of his stripes
and I daydreamed while considering
all those who were yet to die
without caring about
the future or the glory
about time passing like the Seine
under the Pont Mirabeau[8]

I've so often shadowed your ghost
through the mean streets of Auteuil
your saddest neighborhood
dreaming of your poor Anne
when your friends made fun
and when you knew the time had come
to know what you wanted

and when you only suspected
while you hoped for freedom
and you had to make a living
and you squandered it
gleeful as a drummer
and alone all alone.

Guillaume Guillaume hey Guillaume
how you were drawn to the printers' corner
at the rue de Croissant and the rue Montmartre
where you went to watch
like children watch electric trains
the Linotypes your friends
tinkling like little bells
ringing in the last hour "the very last"
when it was time for nightlife
and the stars that showed you signs of life
Guillaume O nightwalker
I retrace your footsteps
your heartaches along the Seine
color of your conscience
when you tried to reach
daybreak
and Billancourt
where you found dawn
setting alight the reinforced concrete Greek temple
and the great pyres
for human sacrifice
of the Forty Hours Devotion
and the withdrawal of the elders
and the weak-hearted.

At last you're tired of this old world at last
and of glory and laurels
and of all that you desired
and that you never had
and that we must never have
neither you nor I.

René Crevel

ONE NIGHT, RENÉ CREVEL and I were walking along the quais of the Seine at the beginning of autumn. René was talking very fast, as he always did. I stopped in my tracks before one of the trees that grace the riverbanks. It had leaves no bigger than hundred-sou coins. The wind, so gentle that we hadn't even noticed it, shook the little leaves, and the tree seemed to tremble.

"There's a tree that's like you," I said to Crevel.

He readily agreed. All in all, I think I was not mistaken.

René Crevel was a trembling creature. He trembled from head to toe—painfully, I should add. Whatever the breeze or tempest that caused it, I knew full well that this trembling was permanent, that Crevel could never stop shaking. He was born rebellious, as others are born with blue eyes.

Even his laugh, so tremendous, so tragic, so unbearable, was a revolt. Intense and quick, Crevel rebelled against those around him as soon as he began to think. I didn't know them well, but his family's behavior was enough to make him furious. And I think that the friendship he showed me ever since our first meeting was triggered because he learned my family was like his, and I too had not been able to resist rebelling.

He was an insurgent. Likeable, pleasant, and always anxious to please, he was also contradictory. He was willing to mingle with "impossible" people, including unbearable snobs. He had no wish to forgo his amusements, and he felt no shame for this dubious company. I know well now that what he sought in these associations was quite naturally the chance to rebel and to express his rebellion.

So as not to cause trouble, I won't name names, for he was incapable of not liking those on whom he bestowed his company. Did he have second thoughts? I don't think so.

I often saw him arrive, fuming, at evening or rather night-time events (he craved nightlife), where he was sure to meet creatures that horrified him. And yet, armed with his smile, he would show them the utmost kindness (I apologize for writing this word which must nonetheless be used in the case of Crevel). But as soon as he had the chance, and sometimes even when he didn't, he would explode and resume trembling with indignation.

When André Breton and I published *Les champs magnétiques*, Crevel was among the first to accept our challenge. Notably, he did not make the mistake of judging this book by conventional literary standards. His contribution to Surrealism from that day forward was considerable.

What I'd wish him to be known for, having observed him many days, is the way, despite his nonchalance and apparent detachment, he remained one of the most honest men of his time. I didn't share all of his tastes, and I admit I sometimes fled some of his more offensive friends. I don't want to say more, but I knew them. But he certainly liked danger, and, without bragging or boasting, he sought "*le dérèglement de tous ses sens*."[9]

He did suffer terribly.

And despite all the friendship that I myself and others bore him, we never succeeded in averting his suffering. He had a gift for suffering and knew it. But this knowledge didn't pre-

René Crevel, c. 1930

vent his pressing forward, with all his nervous energy. Useless to tell him that he was wrong to violently want to be right.

His smile and still more his laugh illustrated this faculty for suffering and, though I scarce dare write it, his will to suffer.

I remember one evening I met him at some friends'—to my great surprise, since I had learned the same day that he had heard, from a suspect source, not about the death of one of his dearest friends but of his ruination, in a highly nasty situation. As soon as I entered the studio where we were meeting for a drink, I heard Crevel's laugh. And all evening he laughed himself breathless, and I couldn't help listening to the laugh, which was truly peculiar. He caught sight of me and not surprisingly reported, "I knew." He simply told me: "I don't dare leave."

And he walked off, to go and laugh horribly in the corner,

where the dreadful people were joking. A few days later, I learned he was sick and wanted to be absolutely alone. I saw him again a month later, but he would not share his sadness with me. He had already set out—hands clenched, lips chapped, dark circles under his eyes—for the abyss that lay in wait for him, its jaws wide open.

Crevel was indeed one of those of whom it can be said that they have lost their illusions. But it did not make him bitter. He knew how to amuse himself, especially about human beings. He was indignant at their weaknesses, yet he rejoiced in their peculiarities, and his admiration for madmen (still more perhaps for madwomen) was extreme. He took pleasure in the company of the cranks and dreamers who were happily fairly numerous in Paris. In this realm he was eclectic. But he knew how to "shrink" them, the way that Indians shrink heads of the dead. I believe at a certain point in his life he even collected those he called "extraordinaries." He preferred to meet them at night, because, he claimed, after twilight they were more sure of themselves.

When he was alone, he was happy to write letters. His handwriting, oversize for his age, was quick and cheerful. Should we hope that someone collects and publishes all the letters he wrote? Even though I am personally opposed to this kind of posthumous exhibitionism, I think one could publish some of the dedications with which he generously embellished his books, in the guise of explanations.

All the same, he preferred to telephone. The role the telephone played in Crevel's life is hard to appreciate. But it was important. René Crevel felt the need to stay in contact with "his people," his friends or his strange companions, but also to always clarify his thinking. No sooner had he ended a conversation than he'd ring up to explain at length exactly what he had meant to say.

If I harp on this proclivity for the telephone (which is not so rare today), it's because it seems to me to illustrate René Crevel's determination never to leave his friendships at a standstill. He couldn't bear not to clear up misunderstandings. And sometimes, because the misunderstanding wasn't cleared up as he wished, he didn't hesitate to fall out (as he put it). But more than misunderstandings, he hated indifference or neutrality. He pushed people to the wall, but wouldn't let himself be cornered. He was ready, moreover, to suffer the consequences of his behavior. But it would be wrong to think that these demands were hard to accept. Crevel knew the secret of being both intransigent and affable at the same time, harsh and engaging and, for some, fascinating.

René Crevel's "charm" has been much discussed, perhaps too much. This vague word, overused and randomly bestowed, does not convey the radiance of the man Crevel. I've asked many of his friends to try to define it, and none could do so. They gave me a lot of reasons, but they all seemed too vague to remember. All I wish to recall is that, from the moment you saw Crevel or spoke to him, you knew you were in the presence of someone different, and I use this word in its strongest sense. He was, it's easy to say now, determined to direct his destiny so as not to succumb to the facile, the banal in literary milieus, to success at any price. But he was capable of dangerously grazing these rocks. Rereading his books is enough to recognize the risks he liked to run: *Détours* or *Babylone*. In *Mon corps et moi*,[10] however, he seemed to want to renounce the tightrope walker's poise, in asserting himself, to shake off the weight of all he had agreed to carry until then. After all, the books he published, as fast as he could, were only dubious reflections of himself. And I'm convinced that he didn't want to attach too much importance to them. He even gladly forgot them, and I had the impression that for him the books were bottles thrown into the sea. He was not a man of messages nor of calls to action. He preferred experimentation, and I believe he took delight in considering his novels in particular not as finely tuned but as trials. Furthermore, thanks to Surrealism, he discovered a realm of wide open spaces that he traveled through alone. He didn't have the time to continue his explorations, but I'm certain it was this activity he would primarily want to be remembered for.

So, despite the uncommon faithfulness of his friends, what is remembered about René Crevel is likely to leave out the very things he held most dear. What is needed is to encompass the entire story of his life.

Marcel Proust

I've always liked people who are called extravagant. Since childhood, when I've had the pleasure to meet women and men who are considered fantastic individuals, I couldn't help speaking to them, while my contemporaries avoided them and fled. One of my most beautiful childhood memories is of a woman, pretty as a paint shop, who was strolling along the streets of the VIIIe arrondissement. She wore a hat with ostrich plumes and metal loops, perched atop a tall wig. Her dress was of puce silk, trimmed with black and white lace and a train that was spotted with mud. She was shod in high patent leather shoes. And glacé kid gloves, of course.

She was truly magnificent. Naturally, I wanted to speak to her but, used to teasing and insults (she was often treated like a freak), she turned her head imperiously and, seeing me persist, smacked me with her handbag. I followed her. She walked at a breathless pace. During this pursuit I noted what a neighborhood celebrity she was, what an aura she had. People stopped to watch her go by. Jean Giraudoux admired one of her rivals and named her *The Madwoman of Chaillot*.

It was in this same period, during my vacation at Cabourg, that I met a man whose singularity attracted me and I wanted, as was my custom, to make his acquaintance. One of my friends, older than I, introduced me to the man, who sometimes strolled through the casino in the evening. His name was Marcel Proust. I felt the same amazement and sympathy as for my strange friend of the VIIIe arrondissement.

Marcel Proust always managed to astonish me. Towards six in the evening, at sunset, a rattan armchair was brought out onto the terrace of the Grand Hotel of Cabourg. It remained empty for a few minutes. The staff waited. Then Marcel Proust slowly drew near, parasol in hand. He watched inside the glass door for night to fall. When they passed near his chair, the bell-boys communicated with signs, like deaf-mutes. Then Proust's friends approached. At first they spoke of the weather, the temperature. At this period—it was 1913—Marcel Proust feared or seemed to fear the sun. But it was noise that horrified him most.

All the hotel guests talked about how Monsieur Proust rented five expensive rooms, one to live in, the other four to "contain" the silence.

Fascinated, I came close for a better look, and he spoke to me because he had heard I was the son of one of his budding young girls.[11] He often talked about dance lessons that took place in an apartment on the rue de Ville-l'Évêque.

"It's there that I met your mother, your aunt—she was named Louise, no? I can see her eyes, the only ones I can say were truly violet."

He spoke quite a bit about his youth, coincidences, encounters, regrets. His smile was young, his eyes deep, his gaze weary, his movements slow. Of course, I was unaware of his writing. He never mentioned his work, even though this was the time when he was writing *À la recherche du temps perdus*. No one, for that matter, seemed to suspect it. He did, however, ask a lot of questions. Sadly, I remember only a few. They seemed childish to me. For instance: "What time of year, exactly," he

Marcel Proust, 1900

asked a waiter in a café, "do the cherry trees bloom in the orchards of Cabourg, not apple trees, cherry trees?"

Another day he summoned one of the hotel cooks to ask for the recipe for Sole à la Mornay. The cook recited it. Marcel Proust slipped him a banknote. And, pocketing the tip, the cook left, murmuring, "It's too much, too much!" Another day, he asked what make of cigar the Prince of Wales, who had become Edward VII, smoked. What do you call a Cronstadt hat?

I couldn't believe it. My jaw would drop, listening to him.

Sometimes you found him seated at a big table. He would offer those who approached a glass of champagne. When he called for cigars for his friends, you knew he was about to leave.

"Excuse me," he'd say. "The cigar smoke makes me cough."

And he would stand up. He seemed to be in a hurry to get back to his room and the silence.

I didn't see him again till a few years later, after the war. I knew he was a writer, since he'd had the kindness to send me *Du côté de chez Swann*. People were starting to talk about him. But he went out less and less. I spotted him one night at the Bœuf sur le Toit.[12] He was terribly changed. I went to say hello and sat down in front of him. He was feverish, overwrought even. He spoke in a low voice. He asked if I had been back to Cabourg. I talked about Cabourg a little. But he seemed so tired that I didn't persist. He withdrew on tiptoe.

A few months later, I sent him the *Les champs magnétiques*, which had just appeared. I was living at this point on the quai Bourbon, on the île Saint-Louis, very near his friends the Bibescos. One evening around eight o'clock, my doorbell rang. A driver asked if I would come speak with Monsieur Marcel Proust, who was waiting in a car outside. I said yes, of course, though I lived only a half flight up. It didn't matter.

Marcel Proust was muffled up in the back of a taxi. His eyes were glowing, like an owl's. He apologized profusely, too profusely for my liking, for having disturbed me.

"I've come from the Bibescos, who are your neighbors."

He would not have wanted to pass my door, he made clear, without thanking me for the gift of a "major" book. (Marcel Proust did not hesitate to employ superlatives.)

"I'm so tired that I can't thank you as thoroughly as I should, and since I wasn't sure of finding you in, I have written you a letter. Here it is."

He suddenly closed his eyes. He seemed exhausted. Was he playacting? I don't think so. I thanked him and took my leave. He had once again succeeded in astonishing me. His extreme courtesy, excessive, was perhaps overbearing.

Later, I wanted to thank him for sending me, in turn, one of his books, but he had his driver tell me that he was too tired to receive me but that he would send word some evening if I wasn't afraid of going out after midnight.

I wasn't the only one who believed that he secluded himself and refused to see those who could have brought back memories he no longer had use for. In truth, and I easily understood it, he was racing to finish his work which was, in any case, never finished, although he understood it was necessary to write "the end" at the bottom of one of the pages of his manuscript.

James Joyce

NO ONE, TO MY knowledge, has subjected his life to his work more than James Joyce. Nor did he accept this bondage of every instant, bondage of body and soul, without suffering—which I witnessed. I can see him, during one of the days I spent with him, tormented by a word, rebelliously constructing a framework, summoning his characters, drawing a hallucination from music, throwing himself, exhausted, onto a divan to better hear this word that was going to be born, that was going to shine forth. Then, for an hour or more, a great silence broken by laughter. At the end of the day, he tried in vain to escape, jumping into a taxi, visiting a friend, having a bit of the dictionary read to him, and, at nightfall, returning home after many a "stopover." He allowed himself one reward, the theater. All around him raged storms, familial or global, financial or social. Stunned to see the world in tumult, cruel or corrupt, he witnessed it the way one of us "attends" a concert. His apparent absent-mindedness was comparable only to that of certain legendary savants. He was the most affectionate, the most tactful of friends and the most distinctive of mine. Yet the people who crossed his path without regarding him, and without his regarding them, spoke only of his absent-mindedness, which they sometimes called egoism.

If I dwell on it, it's because I realize he honored me as a witness to part of his life. When I knew him in 1918, he was writing *Ulysses*. He was known only to a few, but he neither doubted nor marveled at his own genius. He was already giving himself up to this daily damnation, the creation of the Joycean world.

What is most striking about this phenomenon that was, in the scientific sense of the word, one of the purest in literary history, is its unity. Joyce's first work foretold and prepared its eventual full flowering. What will be finally perfected in *Ulysses* is already attempted and approached in *Dubliners*. In these fifteen stories the reader, the author, and the central character are identified. The writer forbids himself to lie. He rejects what we pejoratively call literature. No false attitude, no cheating, no misunderstanding: the most complete good faith.

From the point when he was compelled to write, Joyce abandoned himself entirely to it. All his actions, all his reading, his studies, his joys, and his pain were dedicated to his work. He was the exact opposite of a dilettante.

This experiment, so scrupulously conducted and without a day's lapse, would itself deserve a thorough discussion. It is unique, to my knowledge, in human terms.

This life commands the attitude of readers. It demands the effort to tackle Joyce's work. It restores a different meaning and a dignity to reading that most contemporary novels had denied it.

But it is essential to underscore the value of this nearly 40-year experiment in creating an oeuvre that is one of the highest points in literature.

This body of work, as I've already said, begins with *Dubliners*, continues with *A Portrait of the Artist as a Young Man*, leads to *Ulysses*, and ends with *Finnegans Wake*, published several months before Joyce's death. Alongside the oeuvre, Joyce

James Joyce and Philippe Soupault, 1931

wrote a collection of poems, *Chamber Music*; a play, *Exiles*; and a little book of songs, *Pomes Penyeach*.

Each stage, each book marks an advance, what one dares call an evolution. It's what I've described as a flowering.

So we should remember that, for the reader who is no longer indifferent, but rather engaged with the author, it is important to read *Dubliners* before *A Portrait*, then at last begin *Ulysses*, and end with *Finnegans Wake*. To repeat, Joyce created a world, and this world is accessible to us only if we humbly obey the wishes of the author.

As necessary as this obedience is a knowledge of Joyce's life. It is, in fact, of great simplicity. But it is not well known. The numerous biographies already published are generally true. But there is still lacking in them an element that, for want of a better word, one must call poetry. James Joyce was a poet, a tremendous poet, who was conscious of what poetry meant and who lived by it and for it. All the first part of the life of the author of *Ulysses* is recounted by himself, with an intensity that borders on despair, in his book about adolescence, *A Portrait of the Artist*, and then in the first part of *Ulysses*. James Joyce portrays himself under the name of Stephen Dedalus. His entire development, all the background, all the atmosphere of his future life is fixed with a precision and care that make all further accounts pointless. When Joyce stopped writing his own biography, it was because he deemed it no longer part of his oeuvre. We know that on his departure from Ireland he came to Paris to study medicine, that he passed through Zurich and settled in Trieste, where he was an English teacher for the Berlitz school. This Trieste stage, which began before 1914,[13] is doubtless the most important of his life. He completed *A Portrait*, but it was at this point that he became conscious of the magnitude and importance of his work; it was at this time that he broke forever from our world in order to conceive the Joycean universe.

I have rediscovered the traces of Joyce in this eminently unappreciated city, this city so unfairly overshadowed by its proximity to Venice. (Hadn't even I gone there just to retrace Joyce's past?) On the threshold of Austria, facing Italy—where Stendhal meditated and where Fouché ignominiously died—Trieste is the most beautiful, the most European crossroads in Europe. Joyce lived there for ten years in poverty that amounted to destitution. I visited the building where he started writing *Ulysses*, I walked up and down the streets he frequented, I followed his daily route, I listened particularly to the stories, the ambiance, the cries, the language (one of the most varied, one of the most rich, one of the most "composed" in the world) that Joyce listened to with fascinated attention.

People more learned than I will explain the influence that the Triestine language, and above all the life and the development of this language, had on Joyce's thinking. In my opinion, it was considerable. Trieste also supplied the necessary displacement to Joyce: he felt very far from Ireland, distinguishing none the less the glints and echoes of Dublin, but seeing, sensing, hearing better from afar that city where he had loved and suffered and that was the setting for his entire body of work. Distance gives love overtones and an otherworldly glow.

It would be worth retracing his tracks, step by step, during these years. We are yet aware of only a few episodes. One of them that I am going to recount seems to me remarkably significant and will point out one of Joyce's powers: radiance.

Isolated and unknown, the young Irishman, a novice teacher, had one day as a student a Triestin named Schmitt, about 40 years old. He was an odd, shy man, a lighthearted dreamer, a staunch humorist. He was captivated by his young teacher and imparted Trieste to him, without making much progress in English. In the course of conversation, both admitted they were writers. Joyce read his student's work and immediately understood its unique quality. With the enthusiasm and determination that he brought to protecting and defending his friends (of which there were few), he saw justice done to the man we know as Italo Svevo, whose two works, *The Confessions of Zeno* and *As a Man Grows Older*, have remained for a quarter century the most original and fruitful products of Italian literature.

What strikes me even more is that, despite the exiled Irishman's concentration and the productive suffering that his memory inflicted on him, the force of Joyce's radiance revealed itself. I've noted the prestige, the legend that enveloped his life from the moment his name appeared in print. For my part,

I know I was less affected by the brilliance and splendor of his genius, so suffused with humanity, than by his power to transfigure, his sublime talent for reaching the essential on the first shot.

When Joyce came to settle in Paris, having left Trieste and after a sojourn in Zurich—another crossroads—he was already possessed of certitude. From my first encounter, I was immediately aware of it. When I knew I was going to meet him, I naively thought to compare him. I lived at that time in a milieu of writers. I was not much impressed by literature and its mirages. I saw a living man of intimidating simplicity, unconcerned with the impression he produced. With great facility, but industriously, he was learning Paris. As in Trieste, he had chosen to live in one of those buildings which, he said, are "symbolic." In this way he mixed with the masses, frequenting the little cafés. He listened to people speak. I know that in his neighborhood he was regarded as a phantom. Already, his failing eyesight prevented him from going out alone, almost from living alone. But how he could hear! He claimed to judge people by their voice. I was able to follow his astonishing method and admire his memory. We know the importance he attached to language and the role he assigned it. It would perhaps be too hasty to try to define and even limit Joyce's work by boasting of his virtuosity in this arena. Without doubt, the author of *Finnegans Wake* was an extraordinary virtuoso, but he knew how to make use of, to master, and not be mastered.

In the same way, it was people that interested him. Though he had chosen *Dubliners* as examples, what he focused on was the individual. No one has better depicted this behavior that leads from the particular to the general. So, in *Ulysses* he limited his field of vision to one individual's single day. Going beyond the experimental phase, the author knew how to re-create by the most diverse "means" this human universe of which, in a waking state, we have only the smallest inkling.

To observe gestures and what we might call their harmonics, to read looks, to provoke reactions amounts to only a fraction of Joyce's daily work. To compare and especially to contrast with near or distant memories the living and the dead that form "le profond aujourd'hui"[14]—then withdrawing, to put back in their atmosphere the imaginary beings that mingle with the crowd, to follow their tracks. . . . Can one delimit the work of Joyce the observer, endowed with an irritatingly precise memory? His work provides us a standard by which to measure, both his imagination, which brought him to the point of hallucination, and his power to relive and make others relive.

Do we dare then say that Joyce worked? He "lived" his work. I saw much of him at leisure, what's called leisure. We often went to the theater together, which he loved, like all good Irishmen. He loved theater for theater's sake. I mean he was less attracted by the play than by the atmosphere, the footlights, the follow spot, the audience, the kind of solemnity of the performance hall itself. He preferred opera. When he had decided to attend the theater, he was as excited as a child. He would choose a companion, refuse to dine (I am preparing for a sacrament, he told me, to explain this fasting), and afterward take supper in a restaurant where he had pre-ordered his favorite white wines. At the theater, settled in the front row—this was, one thought, because of his very poor eyesight—he kept watch on the actors' performances and listened to them carefully. Only children can display such rapt attention as Joyce. He was always the first to applaud and call "Encore!" after the grand arias. One night at the Paris Opera, he had the grand aria from

William Tell repeated twice. The singer, it's true, was Irish and one of his childhood friends. Everything pleased him, even the crudest vaudeville. What he apparently sought in these halls was this atmosphere that remains one of the spells cast by the theater. He also found there the unique pleasure of being in contact with the crowd.

It is this same pleasure that he no doubt sought in gathering his friends to celebrate remembrances. He would bring us together to celebrate his birthday, his wedding anniversary, his feast day, Candlemas, Epiphany, Christmas, his various books' publication dates. . . . We generally dined late. There were candles on the table, many white wines, an excellent dinner, a cake with little candles. After dinner, one or another of us would sing, then Joyce himself took his turn at the piano and would, depending on his mood, hum or recite Irish songs, generally always the same ones. This would last at least a good hour. Then it was the turn of his son, who had chosen the profession of singer. Léon-Paul Fargue, when he didn't arrive too late, would elaborate 1890-vintage slangy songs or his previous month's creations. There were often dramas since, in the Irish tradition, we drank heavily. One did not try to leave before it was over, towards three or four in the morning. There were, however, some abrupt departures after "words." Joyce, for the most part, was gay, more rarely gloomy. It took him then an uncommon effort to emerge from this torpor, which had something of a child's unhappy sulk.

When my mood didn't suit the somewhat monotonous atmosphere of these parties, which was often, I wondered what pleasure Joyce could indeed seek or find in them. I know he liked his friends, even a little tyrannically. I know he could and would have only a small number of people, and shunned ceremonial receptions and so-called society. But I'm wrong to argue. In these little gatherings, the author of *Ulysses* wanted only to reconnect. Every creature has an inhuman side, and suffers from feeling on the outside, at a distance from other beings and everyday life. His comrades, jostling him, drawing him close, forced him to their level. That is why he demanded their sincerity, and forbade deference, ceremonies, and snobbism.

In rekindling these memories, I note again that Joyce suffered much from his vocation as a writer. What sensitive being could bear without pain this ceaseless tension, these daily sacrifices, and this work without any leniency for himself? Joyce was of a brutality, a hardness when it came to himself that sometimes surpassed understanding. I had the chance of seeing and hearing him work during the time I was translating with him, or rather he was translating with my help, a bit of *Finnegans Wake*, the Anna Livia Plurabelle episode. These translation sessions lasted three hours. They were exhausting. Joyce was never satisfied with his successes. Nevertheless, I had never encountered a man who was as sure and as accurate a translator. He needed to treat words like objects, to stretch them, dissect them, examine them under a microscope. He went at it fiercely and never gave up. It was not from "conscience" or mania; it was the application of a ruthless method. It concerned a "subject" so moving, so rich, so new, so fleeting also that you could never let up, not even for a second. And I remain convinced that on account of his translation partners Joyce restrained himself, that he took pity on them. When he worked alone he was even more uncompromising. He let himself be flooded by this tide of ideas, plans, memories, comparisons, visions, sounds, descriptions, odors. . . . At the center of this whirlpool, he preserved his sangfroid and his critical sense, dreading the cowardice that makes acceptable the approximate, the almost.

When I want to describe his state while working, I can't avoid the cliché "body and soul." Before my eyes, Joyce, forefinger raised, saying no, rejecting a word, a sentence, criticizing, taking back a fragment, destroying pages already on the verge of being written.

To appreciate his labor and his technique, it is unnecessary to have had, as I did, personal contact with James Joyce. It is necessary and sufficient to read the books. *Ulysses* is perhaps the best example. Each chapter, where not a false note, not a mistake, not a regret is discernible, forms so definitive an ensemble that even an inattentive or unsure reader can't avoid an enchantment that he can neither explain nor resist. Because Joyce requires from his readers an effort that cannot be dissipated. He imposes on them first his tone, his color, his style. Never is the imagination given free rein. From the first word, whoever dares begin reading is as if captured and must, at any cost, bend to the author's will. It is a test of strength. So it's not surprising that so many, from fear, content themselves with admitting, "I don't understand," and adding, "It is too hard for me."

Even if you read with great care, you wouldn't know how to grasp altogether, at first approach, the richness of this work. Thus we are limited to knowing a vast countryside solely by flying over it.

Joyce's singular attitude toward criticism is understandable. You couldn't call it indifference. He was often amused by certain insults and took great pleasure in the efforts by some to make him understood, especially those who were the least familiar with his intent. But the disapproval, the ridicule, the incomprehension, the flattery didn't touch him and taught him nothing. This was from neither pride nor guile, but because he had once and for all decided that it was impossible to turn back. And in spite of his pride, he was often disconcertingly humble. At the end of his life, testimonials of admiration, fervent tributes were lavished on him. He received them very graciously, but he did nothing to prompt them. He could have, if he had wanted to, orchestrated his publicity, since he was savvy and very skillful. He was often invited to go to the United States, which, as in many other realms and for many other writers, was the first country to hail the true greatness of Joyce. He refused. I, who had many occasions to speak about him in all the major American cities, can imagine what a welcome was in store for him and what triumphal celebration would have been organized. He knew it too, but always shied away, despite the entreaties of the numerous Irish people in the United States, who would have greeted him with the enthusiasm they alone can show.

Stranger was his refusal to return to Ireland. Can we say that he loved or didn't love Ireland? His entire oeuvre has Dublin and the environs of Ireland's capital for its setting.

And so each day, each hour of the day, he thought of Ireland, he lived and relived his memories, he traveled through the streets and squares of the city thousands of time in his thoughts, the neighboring byways, he looked at each house, he talked with the inhabitants, he described, painted (and in such detail) the moments and the colors. After his departure in 1905, he never wanted to retrace his steps. Upon the pressing demand of an Irish friend, I asked him one day the reason for his refusal. For answer, he simply looked at me and with his long hand, like a blind man, turned through the pages, which were fragments of the part of his work he was writing at the time. Did I misconstrue his response in thinking that, to complete his work, it was necessary for him not to compare reality and its evocation, not to blur his image of Dublin by any inevitable disillusion.

I can never emphasize enough Joyce's attitude, voluntarily exiled, exiled in order to complete his work. It would have been sweet and exciting, especially for an Irishman, to be welcomed in Dublin, to take revenge after thirty years on those who had made fun of the poor little student going into exile. His work was not completed. That sufficed to stifle his longing.

Many came, in my presence, to bring him news of the country. He remembered one and all and laughed, speaking of old Mr. So-and-so, or Pat, or the mother of X, she who had such a strange nose. . . . He laughed, he laughed, but you could make out in this child's laugh a kind of suffering, a regret, and no doubt remorse.

To finish his work, he had taken refuge in Paris, which he cherished with a particular and touching love. He knew only its ambiance, since his weak eyes and his work prevented long walks or rambles. But he "breathed" Paris and discovered a reason to love it at each stage of his exile. Perhaps you could say that he knew and loved Paris like a song, and God knows how he loved songs. He found a rhythm there that helped him live and work. He was not indeed unaware of the risk of his relentlessness.

Paris helped him to finish *Ulysses*, to write *Finnegans Wake*. Never, to my knowledge, was any other work of this type attempted and completed. *Ulysses* already appeared to be a superhuman undertaking. When you are able to study and read Joyce's final work with the care it deserves, you will be convinced of its extraordinary grandeur. There is no hiding the fact that for today's readers, the difficulty in reading it is very great. One can facilitate reading *Ulysses* with various commentaries. A reader of good will who wants to tackle *Finnegans Wake* must have a guidebook. Only with time will we be able to read this great work if not easily, at least simply. It is so many years ahead of its time. It is the privilege of certain geniuses to be able to outdistance the spiritual and intellectual states of their contemporaries, and there is also a price. . . .

James Joyce was not unaware of being in the vanguard. He did not say, like Stendhal, that he would be understood "later," but believed that he would gain readers only slowly, and he expected from them an effort commensurate with his own. He did not look down on his readers, never seeking to encourage their appetite for what is easy. Nor did he write for the "happy few,"[15] since he didn't consider his books to be reserved for an elite. He ceaselessly enriched his art, imposing on everything that he achieved a rigor and a certitude that precluded hesitation and misinterpretation. Joyce dreaded misunderstandings and approximations. For him, and consequently for his readers, there is no happy medium.

Having explained Joyce's attitude, I would like to be able to suggest a way readers facing his final work might behave. Because it is no longer a question of advice, of commentary, of explication. We know the role that reading it plays for a certain number of human beings; we are not unaware of the influence it can exert. The whole problem of literature and its consequences is posed by Joyce's last work. It is obvious we can't try to resolve it in a few lines, nor even define it in a few sentences. It is important, however, to point out the fundamentals of it. The simplest method we know, the most primitive, is the narrative. It is, to tell the truth, a second-best solution. What Joyce intends and requires of himself is to take hold of the whole spirit and not just propose a few reference points for the imagination. One should not compare this decision with the power of that music which overcomes the spirit and carries it away without a chance to resist. The spirit, it is rightly said, surrenders to the flow of music. Joyce's art imperiously compels attention, the way any poetry worthy of the name must always gain it. The mass, the weight, the volume of all poetry are not measurable. The efforts to succeed in discovering new methods are too rare. In this realm, Joyce's resolve remains unique or nearly so. It is because of this resolve, even more than his success, that we must honor him as a genius.

Georges Bernanos

WHAT FASCINATED ME INITIALLY when I first met Georges Bernanos was his eyes. They were a blue that I had never seen before and have never seen since. And it was his gaze. A direct, sincere, piercing, luminous gaze—a gaze impossible to forget. Next, you listened to him, already fascinated. A booming voice, but a warm voice, friendly, a voice that echoed. And his laugh. A giant's laugh. An irresistible and contagious laugh.

I met him shortly before he published *Sous le soleil de Satan*, at one of those gatherings that remind you of the Saint-Lazare Métro station at rush hour. As always, the buffet was under siege: it was stifling and deafening. I headed for the exit and bumped into a man who, like me, was slipping away. We had already become complicit. I apologized at the doorstep. He apologized. It's at that moment that I became fascinated. I introduced myself. He said his name, which was not yet famous. When I uttered mine, he burst out laughing: "The Surrealist? Indeed!"

He was, I already knew, a militant Catholic, provocative, a member of French Action.[16] I was prepared to detest him. And vice versa. I was an atheist and on the far left. Hopeless. Immediately, however, we hit it off. And I know why. We were both primarily nonconformists. But we did not arrange to meet again. It was a mistake, but especially my mistake. So much time lost, wasted, stupidly wasted.

I ran into him several months later. He had become famous, or nearly so. His genius had been acknowledged—a miracle! But he was mortified by this homage from mediocrities. We met near St. Sulpice. "I'm leaving for . . . I don't know where," he said, and he added, laughing and quoting Baudelaire, "Anywhere, out of the world. . . ." He was incensed. Beside himself. Like me. Exasperated. Like me. It was the time of his first great public revolt: the Spanish Civil War. He was leaving the France that he so admired. But he was the most sincere of men. And he did not want to cheat. He was not able to cheat.

1938-1939—Munich—1940-1941-1942. No commentary. Years of suffering, of shame, of disgust.

On leaving prison,[17] still and more than ever a nonconformist, I was sent on a mission to South America, thanks to some kind friends. And so I touched down in Rio de Janeiro one evening in February 1943. A few days later I found Georges Bernanos seated at the table in a downtown Rio café where he usually worked. Since, he explained to me, he needed the atmosphere, the noise, and the bustle of cafés in order to write. He stayed in contact this way, he said, with anonymous humanity. He was writing fiercely intelligent articles for Brazilian newspapers in which he denounced the cowardice, the idiocy, and the crimes of the Vichy government, the Nazi atrocities, the pharisaical hypocrisy of all countries. Despite the difficulties of exile and the heartbreak of suffering intensely the torments of his brothers, Georges Bernanos had lost none of his eloquence or of his astonishing, prodigious vitality. He spoke with admirable frankness and force. He knew how to laugh (his laugh was profound, if I may put it this way, and I

Georges Bernanos, c. 1930

do wish to put it this way) at all the odious people who dared to speak at this time in the name of France, of the so-called National Revolution[18]—Labor, Family, Fatherland. These three words, this "slogan" uttered in front of him, was enough to bring down his wrath. And the wrath of Georges Bernanos was Homeric, to say the least.

I have often, very often, thought of him after so many years and I have never been able to forget what is feebly and banally called his "charm." So many ideas, convictions, and memories separated us (and we both knew it), and yet we felt, we were sure, that we were once again accomplices. I was amazed at his trust in me when, as was my habit, I told him everything I was thinking. He was somewhat surprised at my vehemence—he, who was the most vehement. I reproached him (that was a bit much) for his indulgence. He, the most intransigent, made fun of my intransigence. He was so completely friendly that I became jealous of his friendliness to the café waiter who diligently brought his café crème, which he only sipped and let cool. We met up almost every day at this café in downtown Rio, a waiting room, a sort of fish tank but so colorless that we had no trouble forgetting its décor. He, seated at his table with his note pad, would write a sentence and then stop to laugh or launch an attack on a Vichy puppet who had made some kind of idiotic remark. Life in Brazil was not easy. He was constantly having to solve problems having to do with his financial situation or with those around him. Even though his friends, Frenchmen in Brazil or Brazilians, always did their best to help him, Georges Bernanos was anxious. He knew, however, how to restore confidence among his friends and show them it was important not to doubt the future. He thus exerted an influence that never failed.

I admired him. He was quite indifferent to this admiration. Nevertheless, he was aware of its intensity and he neither could nor wished to ignore the fact that he was recognized henceforth as one of the greatest writers of his time. He had accepted the responsibility of it. But never did any writer become conscious of his genius more modestly than he. He was the most unpretentious man, the least swell-headed, that I knew. He was also, when a cloud of sadness or care didn't overcome him, the most cheerful and amusing of comrades. He told such funny stories, such witty anecdotes, that you couldn't help bursting into laughter. And he laughed too, like a kid who has played a good joke.

Of course it is impossible to draw a portrait worthy of Georges Bernanos. One can merely suggest a sketch, cite some traits of the astonishing, prodigious person that he was. Nevertheless, I can only remember him with affection. I was going to write (and I do write), with fondness.

I left Brazil with great sadness, on account of him. We had promised each other to meet again when he returned to Paris "after the victory."

I did see him again after his return to Paris, but not as much as I would have wished. Our paths crossed. We ran into each other more by chance than on purpose. So we must choose our memories.

The last time I saw him was on the occasion of a lecture that he had to deliver in the grand amphitheater at the Sorbonne. We met for dinner on the evening of the lecture at a brasserie nearby. He hadn't yet finished drafting the talk. He was anxious and cordial at the same time, tried out language that he was going to use, flew into a passion, then laughed. I had qualms about distracting him from his task. But he insisted on recapturing the companionable atmosphere from the café in Rio de Janeiro.

The lecture was dazzling, and, despite his truculence, his non-conformism produced a great success, a profound success. I didn't doubt (I had never doubted) that Georges Bernanos had been called to play a major role and that he knew how to say and write what was fit to say and write to safeguard human dignity. It's enough for a single being as exceptional, as deeply sincere as Georges Bernanos not to lose faith, despite all the fog (not to say more) that surrounded us and that still surrounds us.

I have never stopped thinking about him. He has remained my friend. And very often, on learning what is happening out in the world and very close to us, I ask myself this question: "What would Georges Bernanos have said?"

Pierre Reverdy

After his discharge in 1916, Pierre Reverdy lived in a rustic little house in Montmartre. You climbed a stairway that reminded you of a ladder and entered a whitewashed room lit by two windows. A large table in front of one of the windows. Some sheets of paper and a big inkwell on the table.

Reverdy would be sitting at his table. It was his kingdom. He would smile. The smile was ironic, suspicious, but fascinating. Then, his eyes . . . Reverdy had dark eyes, sparkling, pitiless, but sometimes revealing a surprising glint of tenderness. His gaze was as disturbing as his smile because it pinned you, like a butterfly pinned to a corkboard.

It was love of poetry that determined him to publish the *Nord-Sud* review. But I believe he would have preferred to remain alone and write, lacking any desire to make contact with other poets. Of course he liked and admired Guillaume Apollinaire, though he criticized him, not unreasonably, for trying to do "too much." He was friends with his neighbor Max Jacob, but he was annoyed seeing that poet putting on an act. He preferred the company of painters to that of poets: Picasso, Georges Braque even more, the sculptor Laurens most of all. I asked him the reason for this predilection. "They lie less," he told me. I was surprised (and wonder why) at some of his preferences. During this period of his life that was so fruitful and that dominated all his work, he truly, naturally enjoyed himself only when he was able to talk "man to man" (*sic*) with a Chilean poet who wrote in Spanish and French, Vicente Huidobro, who was indeed a genuine poet—Reverdy's most loyal disciple—and also with a Spanish musician, the remarkable guitarist Soler Casabón, whom Erik Satie and Ricardo Viñès, his compatriot, admired. Reverdy was also quite tolerant (which surprised and irritated me) of one of his clumsiest imitators, Paul Dermée, whose goodwill disarmed him.

It was Guillaume Apollinaire who encouraged Reverdy to receive me. I knew only a few of Reverdy's poems, but I did read the *Nord-Sud* review. I think what convinced the poet to welcome me was that he wanted to meet a reader (one of the few) of his review. He looked at me the way one regards a strange creature. He hesitated. Was he going to more or less politely show me the door or consent to speak with me? Because Reverdy, at that time, put people into two categories. The first, and more numerous, comprised "impossible" people, the importunate, the bores, the snobs, whom he dismissed without mercy. The second, women or men who were "*sympathiques*." Even before granting me his friendship, he was willing to show me kindness. I made no secret of my admiration, which, though it astonished him, he judged to be sincere. But he didn't give me a chance to talk about it. When it was his turn to speak (and he took the first turn in any conversation), he did not readily relinquish it. When I ventured to agree with him, he cut me off and said most sincerely and without any irony, "Please, let me get a word in. . . ." The only thing to do was to keep quiet. For all that, I thoroughly enjoyed listening to him. Pierre Reverdy was not only a "dazzling conversationalist" (how regrettable, in order to be understood, to have to resort

Pierre Reverdy, 1940

to such worn-out phrases) but also a stunning and spellbinding orator. His voice was very beautiful, deep and warm. His slight Narbonne accent punctuated the sentences.

He also spoke with his hands. Strong, heavy hands, but always graceful. Watching his hands, I sometimes forgot to listen, which irritated him. Because you had to listen to him. And how right he was.

In those years, he talked about nothing but poetry. He neglected the war, the lies, the propaganda, the mud, the blood, the carnage, the absurdities, and the rest. Poetry became essential. It is because of him that I agreed some people should devote themselves to poetry. And he imposed this vocation on me, even though I was tempted to outsmart, to gain power, and to cheat like many of my contemporaries. He taught me purity. He taught me to hate cheaters. And if, though it repels me when speaking of Pierre Reverdy, I feel obliged to write "I" . . . or "me" . . . it is because I was and remain one of the rare witnesses (as he himself told me later) to this period in his life when he tried to define the powers of poetry. At the same time in the same city, a theorist, a faithless disciple of Mallarmé, was doing his best to set artificial limits on it.

Pierre Reverdy had no wish to take notice of such maneuvers. I can't help comparing Pierre Reverdy's attitude with that of the man who called himself a poet and who, sadly, would end up in Anatole France's seat in the Académie française, where he would a little later sing a hymn of praise to Pétain.[19] I am deliberately recalling these memories, contrasting two ambitions, because I want to exalt the dignity of the author of *La lucarne ovale*.[20] He did not set out to be considered a *poète maudit*. He was filled with pride and was perfectly aware of his genius, but he would never have stooped so low as to solicit or prompt admiration or praise. Too proud to be vain, he accepted being ignored or forgotten, even if it was painful. He was not, however, so surprised, when he was editing his review *Nord-Sud*, that young people in love with poetry came to see him. Neither Louis Aragon, nor André Breton, nor I hid our admiration, which he recognized as quite sincere. He trusted us, since he spoke to us at length many a time about what seemed most precious to him, poetry. Many of these observations can be found in a book to which, he assured me, he attached great importance, *Le livre de mon bord* [*My Logbook*], which he didn't publish until 1948. Already in *Nord-Sud* and in *Le gant de crin* [*The Horsehair Glove*], he had defined what he considered essential in his conception of poetry.

He strove to convince us and readily succeeded. He was

convinced. Useless to contradict him or even to argue. He had long pondered the propositions that he threw at us emphatically like a couple of smacks in the face. At this time, Reverdy was dedicating a large part of his life to contemplation. He had chosen to make a living proofreading for a printer of daily newspapers. It was a necessity that he accepted since he had to live, but he never mentioned or took any interest in it. You knew that he had only one urgency: to go home as fast as possible and sit at his dear table. His desire for solitude was intense. Despite the kindness he showed to some of those who were to him only visitors, you had the impression that he wished they would leave. But he liked to talk about his discoveries. He spoke often and extremely well, but these conversations, or rather these monologues, ended up irritating him. He liked reading the poems that his friends showed him but liked even more to critique them and find examples of what to delete. He was not afraid to be severe, without any desire to be mean or cruel. But he never stopped thinking.

What must be remembered, what must be emphasized, is that Pierre Reverdy—for his attitude, for his dignity, for his demands, for his integrity—is one of those rare men that one is proud to have known, to have respected, to have loved.

Blaise Cendrars

Every Wednesday in the spring of 1917, Guillaume Apollinaire would meet his friends about six in the evening at the Café de Flore, near his apartment. Blaise Cendrars "turned up" (to say the least) regularly. I recall the faces of Max Jacob, Raoul Dufy, Carco,[21] André Breton, and several ghosts whose names are best forgotten. The Café de Flore was not so famous at that time as now. One could breathe there, talk without shouting. A provincial atmosphere. Remy de Gourmont used to come read the newspapers.

Blaise Cendrars, fedora askew and cigarette butt on his lip, did not look very happy. I even think he was grumbling. He was taciturn, which seems surprising. Often exasperated, he proposed what I'd call today "taking our business elsewhere." We, since he asked me along, turned our back on the church of Saint-Germain-des-Prés, which he didn't hesitate to condemn as the ugliest church in Paris (and how right he was) to head towards Notre-Dame, which, to my continual astonishment, had always fascinated him. But I didn't argue. Besides, my new friend had already begun to speak, or rather to recount stories that taught me that true isn't always what appears true. My jaw dropping, I listened to Blaise. In 1917 he was in good humor. Like a dancing master, he revealed Paris to a young Parisian.

Because Blaise, you must not forget, was in love with Paris. He had already traveled a lot (and would travel still more) but Paris was his city of choice. He loved its warts, its cankers, its jewels, and especially its atmosphere and nuances.

At this time, he always liked to spend and end (quite late) his evenings in the shadow of Notre-Dame (and not that of the Eiffel Tower, as I had imagined). It is happily impossible to categorize the subjects of our conversations. What a wonderful *toho-bohu* [hodge-podge] (one of the words he loved!). I think I'm faithful to his memory and to my own memories in evoking *pêle-mêle* [pell-mell] (another of his favorite terms) the stories that he proffered.

Who was he in 1917? Truth to tell, I was dazzled, awestruck by this poet—a true poet—who never ceased speaking for me alone and offered me pearls and sparkles, as in fairy tales. And then we would go to dinner at an anonymous café near the rue St-Jacques, where, poetically, with the right words, he dressed a dandelion-green salad in a garlic-rubbed bowl, singing the praises of Parisian cooking. Who was he? Madly cheerful, as strange as that may seem. Impoverished and one-armed, he learned to write again, to light his eternal cigarette with one hand. I didn't know where to go or where he was going. There was no destination at that time. It was the "heroic" period. Every opportunity for him was a good one. That's how he taught me—and I've never been able to forget it—that you have to live poetry before you write it; writing, that was superfluous. I can't help thinking this was the period when Blaise Cendrars most brilliantly manifested his genius. I know that I may be biased, out of friendship and admiration. I believe, nevertheless, that my friend Blaise was among those who endowed so-called modern poetry with all its power. He was irresistible and, in the largest sense of the word, unbelievable. He was

Blaise Cendrars, c. 1925

very sure of himself. He wrote little in this period, brief poems and short prose: *J'ai tué* [*I Killed*] and *Profond aujourd'hui*. At this point in his existence he seemed less interested in the past than in the future. He introduced me to Fernand Léger, with whom he got along wonderfully, although much less well with Picasso, whose shrewdness and cunning put him off, as with Braque, who was too taciturn for his liking, and not receptive. I do recall, however, his enthusiasm for the cinema. Charlie Chaplin, of course! (It was with him that I saw the film that he rightly considered admirable: *Charlot soldat*.[22]) But he wanted a completely different cinema. Before writing it, he told me the story that would become the extraordinary scenario he published a few years later.[23]

I was quite surprised one day when he led me to the rue de Savoie and a bedroom, if I can call it that, where he had amassed what he called his papers. Old newspapers; writing pads covered with notes; drawings by Chagall, some of which he offered to illustrate a poetry collection that I wrote (*Rose de vents*); old rags; drawings by Modigliani; paintings; ancient clocks; pneumatic letters. A collection of bric-a-brac that he never had any idea of organizing. Now and then, he would pick an object or a book, and it would launch a story that I naturally didn't try to interrupt. One day he showed me a railroad schedule from the United States. I don't know why this leaflet prompted him to tell me the story of his uncles, the poem *Le Panama ou les aventures de mes sept oncles* [*Panama or the Adventures of My Seven Uncles*] that he was contemplating. When he published this amazing poem (which seems to me the most "Cendrars" of all his poems), he wanted the book's format and appearance to be that of a United States railroad schedule. He was, I must mention in passing, very interested in typography and everything concerning printing.

He only rarely occupied his rue de Savoie "bedroom" and preferred lodging in hotels, which gave him the feeling of traveling in the world that for him was Paris. He did have some home ports, of which his favorite was doubtless Montparnasse. He met up at the Café de la Rotonde (which has greatly changed since 1917) with those he called his *copains* [pals][24]—a word he liked. He could be the most cordial of men, and as soon as he appeared he was hailed and greeted, since his popularity in Montparnasse was enormous. The painters liked him and had great faith in him. Pascin, Soutine, and especially Modigliani sought his advice, and he did his best to encourage them since, as we know but forget, life for these painters was tough. It was sometimes destitution. Even those who thought themselves clever, especially critics, often proved to be willfully scornful or indifferent. It was in listening to him talk to these painters that I learned to know Cendrars's most brilliant gift: enthusiasm.

He was so lucid. This lucidity was particularly precious at this time of extreme confusion, when one-upmanship was beginning to impose its tyranny on all the writers, artists, and other visionaries. You no longer knew where you were. It was "the beginning of the end" of World War I. Blaise Cendrars, eyes wide open, did his best to comprehend the coming upheavals. Already, he was explaining to us the enormous consequences of the Russian Revolution, recalling memories from his time and travels in Russia.

This period of Blaise Cendrars's life was very fruitful. But it was brief. It seemed he didn't want to prolong it. I sensed he was worried, sometimes annoyed. He wanted to travel and, not inconsistently, to pull back into himself.

He chose to be a solitary, with dignity and with insolence, not breaking with his friends and pals but selecting them. It was later that he distanced himself. I think Dada and Surrealism prompted for him, as for Reverdy, a more decisive isolation. I knew that he suffered from it. And I think it was a pity.

Baudelaire Rediscovered

A HUNDRED YEARS AFTER his death, we wouldn't know how to understand Baudelaire's personality, "transformed by eternity to himself at last,"[25] if we overlooked the influences that he encountered.

Before weighing these influences, however, it is necessary to define some of the poet's limits. Those who admire Baudelaire—who consider him "the first seer," as he was called by Arthur Rimbaud, and who know he was the precursor of the revolution that sparked the rebirth and liberation of French poetry at the end of the nineteenth and the beginning of the twentieth centuries—are always surprised at the difficulty Baudelaire had in breaking free from the formulas, the rules, the forbidden. We should recall, for example, the dedication of *Les fleurs du mal*:

TO THE IMPECCABLE POET
TO THE PERFECT MAGICIAN OF FRENCH LETTERS
TO MY DEAR AND REVERED
MASTER AND FRIEND
THÉOPHILE GAUTIER
WITH A SENSE OF
THE DEEPEST HUMILITY
I DEDICATE THESE SICKLY FLOWERS
C.B.

Thus Baudelaire acknowledges very clearly and humbly his admiration for the author of *Émaux et camées* [*Enamels and Cameos*], whose critical work—more than respectable—is unjustly forgotten, and this personage who, from the red vest of the Battle of Hernani[26] until the more prophetic visions of his final years, played an important role in the nineteenth century, but who remains no less the representative of the art-for-art's-sake aesthetic, the defender of the strictest prosody and versification in renouncing the seductions of Romanticism in the sphere of poetry. The poet of *Les fleurs du mal* recognizes by his respectful dedication at the start of his literary life that he has sincerely accepted the influence of Théophile Gautier. He will struggle more or less consciously to break free, painfully, from this influence. He will not succeed until he begins to write prose poems, which he will publish under his chosen title, *Le spleen de Paris*, a revealing title whose meaning has not been emphasized enough.

Baudelaire had first thought of titling this collection *Le rôdeur parisien* [*The Parisian Prowler*], a title even more revealing than *Le spleen de Paris*. We know—he often boasted of it—that throughout his life Baudelaire traversed the streets of Paris, "prowled" them day and night, sometimes the lucid observer, sometimes a dreamer habitually haunting artificial paradises. Not as a historian did he wish to know the mysteries of this city that he never left without regret, but as a lover who cherishes even the flaws of his mistress. He preferred Paris "landscapes" to Parisians, whom he disdained and sometimes hated. In the streets of Paris, Baudelaire sought solitude, but in surroundings that suited him. He usually accepted being a spectator, and he remembered various encounters, several of which were vitally important to him. Jeanne Duval, for example, whom he "encountered" in a small cabaret "theater." Théodore de Banville

Charles Baudelaire, Nadar, 1855

maintained that she was roaming the streets. Baudelaire and Jeanne Duval wandered together, searching out shadowy cul-de-sacs and the nocturnal mysteries of deserted neighborhoods. The impressions and echoes of these excursions can already be found in *Les fleurs du mal*, a section of which is titled "Tableaux Parisiens." They are evocations or memories of hospitals, palaces, beggars, old men, scenes, old books, outskirts, little old ladies, blind men, gambling houses, departure points for meditation, excuses, allusions but rarely descriptions. Baudelaire is more sensitive to atmosphere and ambiance than to direct impressions and historical details. He doesn't describe. He evokes. He suggests more than he depicts. It is a whisper that bears out the poet's decisions.

It is difficult, if not impossible (numerous Baudelaire specialists have tried in vain) to map the routes of the man who wanted to be, and who was, a prowler of Paris. One alone we can specify, perhaps, because he made numerous allusions to it, the one that took him along the banks of the Seine, "scenting at every corner the chance of a rhyme." It's in the "old quarter" that he writes his poems, "tripping over words like paving stones / bumping into long-dreamed-of lines."

From the time he writes *Les fleurs du mal*, Baudelaire agrees to acknowledge his debt. He devotes to the Parisian landscape, to his Parisian dreams, poems of a very melancholy beauty, which conclude with these lines:

> *Dawn shivering in her pink and green robe*
> *Advanced slowly along the deserted Seine*
> *And somber Paris, rubbing its eyes,*
> *Took up its tools, like an old workman.*

Baudelaire was "enchanted" by Paris. More than his memories of childhood or travels, it was Paris that inspired him. Obviously we can't create an accounting or derive the source of a poet's inspirations. Baudelaire has, however, revealed one of his secrets to us. It's astonishing that the many commentators and Baudelaire scholars have not emphasized the importance of the poet's evolution—metamorphosis, one could even say. Arthur Rimbaud understood the essence and the necessity of this evolution. In a letter from May 15, 1871—scarcely four years after Baudelaire's death—addressed to his friend Ernest Delahaye, the poet of *Saison en enfer* writes, "But since inspecting the invisible and hearing the unheard-of is different from recovering the spirit of dead things, Baudelaire is the first seer, king of poets, *a real god*. And yet he lived in too artistic a world; and the form so highly praised in him is trivial. Inventions of the unknown call for new forms. . . ."[27] We should underscore such discerning judgment ("call for new forms") and be amazed that Rimbaud neglected in his statement—which is altogether an avowal, a wish, and a confession of such importance as to be emphasized—one of the keys to Baudelaire's work and one of the explanations for what Jean-Paul Sartre was not afraid to call his failure. In his dedication to *Le spleen de Paris*, Baudelaire wrote, after having long weighed the terms of this statement: "Which of us, in his moments of ambition, has not dreamed of the miracle of a poetic prose, musical, without rhythm and without rhyme, supple enough and rugged enough to adapt itself to the lyrical impulses of the soul, the undulations of reverie, the jibes of conscience."[28]

It's astonishing, but one is always astonished studying Baudelaire's official, exterior, social life, that he dedicated his wonderful (and wonderful-seeming to us) prose poems to Arsène Houssaye. Who was Arsène Houssaye? A prolific writer, a clever and ambitious man, and one whom we would call an arriviste. He got himself appointed manager of the Comédie Française, thanks to Rachel.[29] But he was also capable of appreciating what was new. It is likely that Baudelaire sensed that this "Parisian" understood better than the poets he associated with, Théophile Gautier or Saint-Beuve, the poetry he dreamed of and wished to be able to present. In this same dedication, indeed, he defines and gives a strange reason for his need to create poems in prose: "It was, above all, out of my exploration of huge cities, out of the medley of their innumerable interrelations, that this haunting idea was born."[30] We must understand "huge cities" to mean Paris, the only "huge" city that Baudelaire ever knew.

That the influence of Paris was crucial to Baudelaire's poetic evolution, that the "intimacy" with this city convinced Baudelaire to break free of the aesthetic of Théophile Gautier and his imitators, appears incontestable after almost a century of study, research, and meditation on the poet's work.

In order to measure the extent and depth of this revolution (taking the word in every sense), it is necessary at least to try to clarify what Baudelaire's poetry represents (and what it represented for him, more or less consciously). Because the echo of this profound voice, which remains mysterious despite all our attention, has reached us as an imperative, from the near or distant past, as if space and time were suddenly abolished. No doubt it is too powerful for us to want to analyze it. We must conceive and imagine a totally different universe from that of our daily life, but which nevertheless would have the same rapport as that which links two planets, the reflection from one lighting the other. The poetic universe thus lit by the universe where we pass, or where we undergo our life, necessarily has other laws. The rough picture of this universe is given to us by dreams, by what the poet modestly called daydreams, or by visions. We have only a weak and uncertain knowledge of this dream world, according to Baudelaire, who was subject as well to other laws and to the poetic universe. Poetry is in a way illuminated by life, and vice versa, but this reciprocity creates interferences and correspondences.

More or less consciously, Baudelaire suggested that it was the influence of Paris that made him discover the need for his escape, his liberation, which in a way obliged him to renounce the crutches of prosody and traditional versification. He recognized that it was reading Aloysius Bertrand's prose poems that prompted this discovery of a form "rugged enough to adapt itself to the lyrical impulses of the soul." Certainly Aloysius Bertrand, who lived at the time of the triumph of Romanticism, can be considered a precursor, but he was only an intermediary for Baudelaire.

"I have a little confession to make," he said in the dedication. "It was while leafing through, for the twentieth time, at least, the pages of the famous *Gaspard de la nuit* of Aloysius Bertrand (has not a book known to you, to me, and to a few of our friends the right to be called famous?) that the idea came to me of attempting something in the same vein, and of applying to the description of our more abstract modern life the same method he used in depicting the old days, so strangely picturesque."[31]

Thanks to *Le spleen de Paris*, one can trace Baudelaire's steps in the new poetic realm that he was going to explore—not without trepidation.

An outline of a poem was found in his papers after his death, a draft *Dedication to the City of Paris*, which Baudelaire considered putting at the beginning of *Les fleurs du mal*, that ends with this very Hugoesque line:

You gave me your mud and I made it into gold.

This draft dedication reveals the poet's feelings toward the city that he loved passionately, all the while denouncing its flaws but exalting its beauty and its power. His love led him to dramatize and exaggerate. Here, he did not succeed in breaking free of Romanticism. It is indeed hard to allow oneself to be guided by someone who regarded *his* city as a mistress whom he only stopped reproaching and insulting long enough to declare his passion and love for her.

In remembering his walks, in recalling a street scene he observed, Baudelaire does not wish to describe it. Scene, vision, or memory are the departure points for a dream that he writes in the form of a poem, but a *liberated* poem. The words are no longer chosen to comply with prosody but to evoke as harmoniously as possible a state of mind or, even more often, a state of soul. He cannot be a painter. He wants to be the poet who suggests, who dreams and who intends to make us dream. The first poem in *Le spleen de Paris* establishes a mood. As paradoxical as it may seem, it is called "l'étranger" [the stranger]. But Baudelaire gives the word *stranger* a new meaning: for him the stranger is he who is not of this world, who loves neither his father, nor his mother, nor his sister, nor his brother, nor his country, nor beauty, nor gold, but who loves "the clouds . . . the clouds that pass by . . . over there . . . over there . . . the wonderful clouds."

Baudelaire did not agree to and then conceive the prose poem right away. The method, even for a writer of his generation and education, was questionable. You have the impression, reading the first pages of *Le spleen de Paris*, that the poet who knew the rules and craft of prosody and versification as well as Théophile Gautier or Théodore de Banville was threatened by or, even more, frightened of the freedom offered by this new form that he had chosen. You sense him hesitant, worried. But he is certain of having discovered his true mode of expression. At first, he tries to deceive himself. The poet, the seer, does not want to give way to what he still considers facile, because it no doubt seems easy to him, too easy, to write without "crutches." He is set free but his freedom is accompanied by vertigo. At this time in his life, at this turning point, he feels alone. He fears not being taken seriously. Sainte-Beuve (who considered Béranger the leading poet of his time), Sainte-Beuve whom he so admired and from whom he hoped for understanding, and the Académie française, which he hoped to join—neither would or could accept this liberation of poetry nor the emancipation that it entailed. This veritable anxiety on Baudelaire's part explains why he didn't dare quantify the importance of the discovery that he had, in a sense, been obliged to make.

Slowly, poem after poem, at a stealthy (or a poet's) pace, Baudelaire will explore this new world. He describes the scene less and less, and endeavors to create, to suggest and then impose an atmosphere. He is going to discover the poetry of dreams. He even sets himself challenges, since he rewrites "in prose" some poems from *Les fleurs du mal*: "La beauté," "Les petites vieilles," "Hémisphère dans une chevelure," " L'invitation au voyage," "Le crépuscule du soir." He calls up his bygone dreams to better express them. Each prose poem that is like a new version of the most beautiful poems of *Les fleurs du mal* demonstrates that Baudelaire had finally accepted the imperative of his liberation. In one of the last poems in *Le spleen de Paris*, he agrees to escape once and for all when he cries, "At last my soul explodes! 'Anywhere! Just so it is out of this world!'"[32]

Arthur Rimbaud heard this cry that Baudelaire wanted first to shout in the language of Edgar Allan Poe: "Anywhere out of this world." It is very much the demand of *Illuminations*. But the "Parisian prowler" never stops looking for new suggestions in his exploration of Paris. Titles of poems to be written have been found among his rough drafts, titles that explain in some sense the poet's hesitation, which he filed in the category "Parisian items (simple)."

After these projects Baudelaire had decided to transpose what he called dreams, grouping them under a word that was taken and adapted by Guillaume Apollinaire, *Oneirocritée,* which is to say, the art of interpreting dreams.

Unfortunately, Baudelaire left only the titles of these "dream poems" that he wanted to write. Judging by the titles, we can assume that it was not a question of the poet's attempting description or even offering allusions. We can imagine Baudelaire's meditations from these notes, after his discovery not only of a new technique but of a different concept of poetry. Nothing but plans, of course, nothing but intentions are noted. Is it because he was frightened by the extent and consequences of his discovery, by the fresh scandal he feared to cause (after that of *Les fleurs du mal*), and because his health had begun to fail and because serious financial worries obsessed him, that he didn't take or didn't want to take this new and decisive step?

These notes discovered in Baudelaire's papers after his death demand our attention and reflection. They confirm, if there was any need, that the poet of *Le spleen de Paris* had accepted and acknowledged that poetry was, as he had himself also foreseen, the "sister" of dreams. So in order to best understand both Baudelaire's evolution and potential influence, we must reread one by one the titles chosen for *Oneirocritée*, titles that critics and numerous expert commentators on Baudelaire's work, life, and evolution seem to have neglected or at least underestimated in importance.

These are the dreams, or nightmares. *Symptoms of Ruin. My beginnings. Back to High School. Strange apartments (places known and unknown, but recognized, dusty apartments; house moving; rediscovered books). Landscapes without Trees. Death Sentence (so forgotten by me, but suddenly remembered since the sentencing). Death. The Mousetrap. Festival in a deserted city (Paris, night, at the time of the Italian War). The Palace by the sea. The Staircases (vertigoes, great curves,[33] hanging men; a sphere, fog above and below). Prisoner in a Lighthouse. A Desire.* (Capitalization is Baudelaire's.)

It would, of course, be dangerous to draw too hasty a conclusion from studying each of these titles. All the same we can accept the suggestions and recognize the new direction the poet wanted to embark on. When he made these notes to arrange and preserve the plans he dreamed and thought about, Baudelaire was going through a particularly critical period. He experienced anxieties that were understandably frightening and crises of despair whose depth some of his letters of the time reveal. Little known as he thought himself to be (not without reason), it is likely the poet no longer had complete confidence in himself. One supposes that he doubted his genius. His increasingly failing health did not allow him to overcome the depressions he was already complaining of in his prose poems:

> And going home at that hour of the day when Wisdom's counsels are not silenced by the roar of the outside world, he said to himself: "I have possessed in dreams today three homes and was equally happy in all of them. Why should I drive my body from place to place when my soul travels so lightly? And why carry out one's plans, since the plan is sufficient pleasure in itself."[34]

In order to accept this dream of the poet that the difficulties and worries of everyday life were closing in on all sides, we must remember that he had become a vagabond, wandering Paris from hotel to hotel. He still tries to write, but experiences great difficulty from then on in collecting his thoughts. We know from hearing his admissions and sad confessions that he no longer has the strength to contest his fate. But, and it is then that we can admire his genius without reservation, then that he becomes the visionary that Rimbaud saluted so enthusiastically. At the end of his life, when he wrote the most beautiful and significant of his prose poems, he is no longer the scholar, the technician, the versifier of *Les fleurs du mal* and the admirer of Théophile Gautier. He discovers, at last accepting his discovery, the very essence of poetry.

But at the same time (1862), he felt "the wing beat of imbecility" pass over him. He no longer dares break free permanently. It is what has been called the tragedy of Baudelaire, that of a stricken genius who can no longer ignore that he is condemned. "On borrowed time," the poet will experience only flashes of lightning. We can follow in the posthumous notes this struggle between "imbecility" and genius. Poetry became for Baudelaire a series of illuminations followed by periods of darkening. The "illuminations" of the final period, however, are more revealing than the assertions and declarations from the time when the form of the poems in *Les fleurs du mal* was the constant subject of preoccupation. In truth, Baudelaire no longer represents. Is he still able? He no longer has time to debate. He can only seek the sole deliverance that still permits him to escape darkness, silence, the final plunge. He wants to try to discover the essence of poetry. But he can only grope forward. Even the prose poems of *Le spleen de Paris* can no longer satisfy him, because he had already agreed to the pretexts. He succeeded, however, in making himself understood. One who has studied his prose poems most closely and who has tried with utmost wisdom to characterize their spirit and their scope is Henri Lemaître, the editor of the most recent edition of *Le spleen de Paris*. In his preface to this collection, which is both a subtle and erudite analysis of this work that was too long misunderstood, he writes,

> Memorable example of poetic achievement . . . He fully realized in it his ideal of magical modernity . . . and the intersection under the sign of supernaturalism of the extraordinary and the quotidian. . . . The prose poems attempt another avenue of expansion in poetic magic, in the direction of effacement of form, strictly speaking, in the aid of spiritual music and atmosphere (in the sense that painters, and particularly landscape painters, understand the term): getting at

the intimacy of the unusual, at the strangeness of the present, or reciprocally, at the closeness of the dream, at the fantastic actuality—such is the objective of the prose poem, where postulations and languages, impressions and experiences, marionettes and heroes, former life and life today, entwine with the presence of the poet and his writing, for a living skeleton.

The poet's intentions are thus fixed. The poetry that he "foresaw" is at last accepted. The poet's solitude, that of the seer, is understood. We penetrate the universe that he had discovered and agree to follow him, eyes open, senses vigilant.

Beyond *Le spleen de Paris*, which incidentally didn't appear until three years after Baudelaire's death, it is against the same dread of the unknown, of the unusual and the infinite, that the poet must fight. He explores then and for several years, his last years, like a blind man groping, but also like a seer, the realm that he was the first French man of letters to reach. So it is very much he who pointed the way to the new.

Henri Rousseau, le Douanier

UNFORTUNATELY, I NEVER KNEW him. It's one of my great regrets. But I always considered him one of my friends. When I first saw a painting of his in 1916 (it was a little Seine riverside landscape), I learned the artist was dead but that a number of writers and painters had known him. I went to interview them and, despite some unintentional false evidence and contradictions, I succeeded in drawing for myself a portrait of Henri Rousseau, known as le Douanier [the customs officer].

Since that period, I have happily followed this painter's rise, the phenomenal rise that was celebrated in 1962 by an exhibition of almost all his work. But despite this "triumph," no one has succeeded in dispelling the misunderstanding surrounding Henri Rousseau. The best-intentioned art critics have called this great painter, this pioneering artist, primitive, and there has been no hesitation to use the word in the sense of simple-minded. "Sunday painter," said other similarly misinformed critics. This was a serious mistake and an injustice that, despite the efforts of many, has not been corrected. The main reason for this grave misunderstanding is that no one has yet tried to depict the true personality of Henri Rousseau.

He was a pleasant and engaging man, but proud. His pride, which revealed itself unashamedly, made some of the painter's best friends think that he was conceited, others that he was mad, and others (less discerning) that he was stupid. But what was more serious, the first to assess the importance of Rousseau were pranksters. Alfred Jarry, first of all, who "introduced" his fellow citizen, never failing to do it like *Ubu*; and then Guillaume Apollinaire, who couldn't help ridiculing those who laughed at le Douanier and then spoofing them.

But in hoodwinking them, he couldn't avoid misleading the painter, who was only too inclined, with good reason, to take seriously what was said, even the most insulting commendation. Recall—and it is only one example—the "Rousseau banquet," whose story is told in *Les soirées de Paris* by Maurice Raynal, a dauber's banquet in Picasso's studio (another practical joker).

It's astonishing to us in 1962 that the canvases Rousseau exhibited at the end of the nineteenth century were met with laughter. It is easy, however, to recall the reception a few years earlier that met the works of Manet, Cézanne, or Van Gogh.

Henri Rousseau began painting at a time when a revolution was breaking out in the world of painting. And before this revolution was over, before its consequences had been accepted, he announced a new revolution. The backlash didn't take long. It confronted Rousseau's revolution with the most treacherous weapons: irony, laughter, insults, refusal to honestly consider what he presented.

With the help of his friends a legend was created. Henri Rousseau, it was said repeatedly, was a naïf, a bit of a clown. The Belle Epoque critics, who were nobody's fools (it was obvious) were only too happy to find a butt for their jokes. They didn't even take the trouble to look at his canvases. They were amused, and ridiculed them. Henri Rousseau didn't deign even to respond to those who made fun of him. He knew he was a great painter.

*Henri Rousseau,
self-portrait, 1890*

We possess a document that justifies the repudiation of such a false legend. It is a note that the painter himself composed in 1894. That year, a publicist, Girard Coutance, published a work titled *Portraits du prochaine siècle* [Portraits of the Next Century]—which was not, upon reflection, a bad title—dedicated to the poets and prose writers of the period, comprising two hundred biographical notes signed by Stéphane Mallarmé, Charles Morice, Roger Marx, Jacques des Gachons, Franz Jourdain, V.-E. Michelet, Léon Bloy, Paul Verlaine, Henri de Régnier, and Jules Renard.

A second collection concerning painters and sculptors was bound to follow. Rousseau, having gotten word of the project (we must see in this a sign of his natural pride), went one morning to the workshop where they were preparing to print the artists' "portraits," to bring his pen-and-ink self-portrait, depicting himself "with his bushy beard and sorrowful expression," and with the portrait this biographical note:

> Born at Laval in 1844: given his parents' lack of wealth, was obliged to follow at first another career besides the one to which his artistic tastes called him. It was not thus until the year 1885 that he made his debut in Art, after many setbacks, alone, with no other teacher than nature, and a little advice received from Gêrome and Clément. His first two pieces exhibited were sent to the Salon des Champs-Elysées; they were titled: *Une danse italienne* and *Un coucher de soleil.* . . . [*An Italian Dance* and *A Sunset*]
>
> After many severe trials he succeeded in becoming known by a number of artists who surrounded him. He perfected himself more and more in the original style that he adopted and is becoming one of our finest realist painters.

This brief autobiography will make the true significance of his work understood. We must realize how this self-portrait in fact makes clear that the "customs officer" was never an amateur and still less an amiable humbug. Henri Rousseau's vocation was stronger than the influence of his milieu, than the hatred for what is new, than poverty—since we mustn't forget that in order to buy canvas and paint, le Douanier never in his life ate his fill, as has been shown in letters that were found. Neighborhood merchants from time to time took pity on the person they called "the dauber." The painter at times gave lessons and "took" portraits of his neighbors for a mouthful of bread or simply to please. It wasn't until the end of his life that Henri Rousseau received some rare encouragement, and the warmest and most perceptive was that of Guillaume Apollinaire. "Rousseau," the poet told me when I interviewed him, "was the most conscientious painter that I ever knew. He was very obstinate, and if he listened attentively to the advice he was given, he never followed it. He didn't like to talk about his past. He preferred to talk about his work and his plans. His friends knew that he was amorous, eager for affection, but he never introduced us to his sweethearts. Just one time he asked me to write a testimonial certifying that he was a reputable painter, with real talent. He was a very good man, always ready to help his friends, to the extent of his modest means. He was very poor. . . ." Another witness at the end of le Douanier's life, Jérôme Tharaud, told me that the painter was "kind," with a disarming courtesy, but he spoke of his paintings with excessive gravitas. He didn't even realize that he was sometimes being kidded, as was the custom. You had the impression he wouldn't accept not being taken seriously for even an instant. More mistrustful, Maurice Raynal claimed that le Douanier was sly (he was apparently quite proud to be described as a customs officer even though he had only worked for the municipal toll service). "He gladly accepted praise but was deaf to critics and refused to respond to questions put to him about his paintings. He had what was not yet called a sense of humor. He gave the impression of living 'in another world.' He was interested only in his painting and in his personal life, in his love affairs. He was a dreamer. Robert Delaunay told me that Rousseau had an incomparable technique."

We also need to mention the statement of Mme. Fernande Oliver, who was Picasso's companion and often received Rousseau at her house towards the end of his life. She recounts that, leaving the Indépendants exhibition, Rousseau said to Picasso, "In short, you and I are the two greatest painters of our time. You in the Egyptian style, I in the modern style." Maybe we shouldn't attach too much importance to these accounts. All those who knew him, however, have told me that Rousseau was afraid of ghosts. He claimed in all seriousness—and it is this manner of assertion that prompted critics not to take him seriously—that when he was painting, ghosts came to encourage or criticize him and even wake him at night, "tugging at his feet," to make him continue painting, to finish one of his canvases. One can imagine that what Rousseau called ghosts, other painters would call remorse or scruples.

Without a doubt, Henri Rousseau took himself seriously, and we now know that he is the one who was right. Without weighing its consequences or harm, he had accepted the role of a somewhat ridiculous and pitiable person that even his best friends visited on him and that journalists, eager for the colorful and ironic, exploited without shame.

Maybe it is because I always considered Henri Rousseau a friend that I never accepted the distortions, the burdens of this myth, and that I have always protested. In vain, no doubt. Despite the painter's "triumph," even though dealers sell the most questionable works of Rousseau for their weight in gold (even more), while numerous studies and respectable books have been devoted to him, he has not yet ceased being considered a sad case, a self-taught naïf.

We know, of course, that Rousseau was a simple man, but we must give this word all the nuances that are due. What is surprising, when one tries to study his life and his personality, is that his contemporaries, except for a few rare friends, couldn't figure out that Rousseau's simplicity didn't prevent him from being a great painter—far from it.

Always too late, it is high time to do him justice. It is impossible to think of the end of le Douanier's life without sadness. During his last years, he began selling canvases for amounts that seem ridiculous today, but that for him meant the end of poverty. He could then paint the grand compositions that are his masterpieces.

But if he noticed that a few rare connoisseurs finally did him justice, he was suffering from solitude. Still romantic—one of the secrets of his genius—he was smitten by a widow. She was heartless, made fun of Rousseau and even refused to be adored. It was said she took the painter "up the garden path," and he complained of being stood up regularly. Very self-centered, she accepted presents from Rousseau that, for her part, she didn't take seriously. If she had known the prices that her admirer's paintings were going to fetch, she would certainly have changed her attitude. She treated him like a clown. Rousseau, who never doubted his genius, didn't dare vaunt it, for fear of being put painfully in his place (this was how he described the shrew's tantrums). He never got over the widow's terrible rebuffs.

So on the brink of death, the "kind" Rousseau thought about painting and love but did not forget about liberty. As he sometimes liked to do, he had noted by way of a caption for one of his compositions, *Le Dernier du 51e*, this wish: "O liberty, be always the guide for those who by their labors would contribute to the glory and the greatness of France."[35] But when he died on September 2, 1910 at the Necker hospital, the attendants at his last throes treated him like some old alcoholic. Seven people, his neighbors, followed his coffin.

And the myth that portrays him as a mental case, a clown, and a simpleton is not yet demolished.

Remembering Philippe Soupault

by Ron Padgett

"Really, you should meet him, just to shake hands and say hello."

My friend Serge Fauchereau was trying to convince me to do something I've always resisted: to meet my literary gods. I had fallen for Philippe Soupault's work when I first read it, in 1963, at the age of 21, especially the charming early poetry, the hypnotic *Last Nights of Paris*, and the explosive *Magnetic Fields*. Two years later, living in Paris, reading and translating some of Soupault's work for my own pleasure, I dared not even send him a postcard across town.

And so finally, about 12 years after that, I found myself sitting in a booth in the Café Apollinaire on the boulevard Saint-Germain, with my 10-year-old son to my right, Fauchereau facing me, and Soupault across from my son. We began the conversation in French, but Soupault quickly suggested, "Let's speak English. The boy doesn't understand French, no?" The gentle diplomacy of his manner and the consideration he showed for my son dispelled my concern about meeting a "great man." I was meeting a real man, one who showed no trace of loftiness, pretention, or condescension, and who, like an ideal grandfather, was happy to share the conversation with all three of us on an equal basis.

In the course of the conversation, Serge mentioned *Last Nights of Paris*. Soupault seemed surprised when I told him how much I liked that work, which I had read in the Rare Book Room at Columbia University, in the translation by William Carlos Williams. When Serge suggested that I publish a new edition of it, at the small press I co-directed, I replied that I would be thrilled to do so. We looked at Soupault. "It sounds delightful," he said with a happy smile.

No discussion of money, contracts, or publicity. Just a straightforward sense of delight. And in fact that meeting proved to be typical of all my dealings with Soupault: he was generous, cordial, and enthusiastic, and he never made anything more complicated than it had to be. Now I understand why two of his mentors, Cendrars and Reverdy, who could be rather thorny at times, preferred Soupault's company to that of his young Dada and Surrealist colleagues.

Soupault's personal manner was a reflection of the lightness of touch of his best poems, a delicacy that is so artful that it never calls attention to itself. Given substance by his human decency and his willingness to explore some rather far reaches of the mind, this deft touch enabled Soupault to express a quietly radiant happiness and a palpable affection for the world. It is all these things that continue to make him a model for a small but devoted number of American poets in each new generation who are looking for a type of inspiration they can't easily find in their own country.

When the waiter brought the check, Soupault, even at an advanced age, was quicker than the rest of us. "On me," he said. He looked at the total and said to the young waiter, in a wry, gentle voice, "You know, Apollinaire himself would not have been able to afford this café." And then he left a big tip.

Notes

1. Francophone readers seeking more information can consult Soupault's *Vingt mille et un jours* (1980) and the two-volume *Mémoires de l'oubli* (1981 and 1986).

2. Rolland was a pacifist.

3. *Nouveau* preceding a noun means "new," while following a noun it means "the latest."

4. Reference to Chateaubriand's "longed-for tempests."

5. According to Gabrielle Buffet-Picabia's "memories" in Robert Motherwell's *The Dada Painters and Poets*, *391* was, in fact, edited, published, and largely created by Picabia, with contributions from Ray, Duchamp, and others, and was intended to recall the earlier *291*, published by Alfred Stieglitz and three associates, a renaming of the Stieglitz magazine *Camera Work* for his 291 Gallery in New York located at 291 Fifth Ave.

6. Refers to Apollinaire's *Le flâneur des deux rives* [Wanderer on Both Banks] published in 1918.

7. In 1911 the 30-year-old Apollinaire had been jailed for several days in connection with the investigation into the theft of the Mona Lisa and other art objects from the Louvre. Although Apollinaire was familiar with the thief of two Iberian stone sculptured heads and their sale to Picasso, and helped effect their restitution, he was apparently not involved in the theft of the Leonardo painting, despite a persistent legend to the contrary. Picasso's behavior in the affair was criticized by Apollinaire's friends. See Francis Steegmuller's *Apollinaire, Poet among the Painters* for a carefully researched account.

8. See "Le pont Mirabeau" in *Alcools*

9. "Derangement of all his senses" refers to Rimbaud's often quoted prescription for seeing into the unknown.

10. *My Body and I* explores the tensions between body and spirit.

11. Reference to *A l'ombre des jeunes filles en fleur*, book two of *A la recherche du temps perdu*.

12. The Ox on the Roof, Paris nightclub, opened in 1921.

13. Joyce lived mainly in Trieste from 1904 until he sought refuge in Zurich in 1915 during World War I.

14. Reference to "Profound Today," Blaise Cendrars's 1917 prose poem.

15. Stendhal dedicated the first book of *The Red and the Black* to "the Happy Few."

16. Action française, a right-wing monarchist movement founded in 1898 during the Dreyfus affair.

17. Soupault was imprisoned for six months in Tunis during the Vichy regime.

18. The ideological name under which the Vichy government was established in 1940, which also replaced the Republic's motto—Liberté, Égalité, Fraternité—that dated from the 1789 French Revolution.

19. Paul Valéry was elected to Analole France's seat in 1925. Marshal Pétain was chief of state of Vichy France.

20. Reverdy's second book, *The Oval Skylight*, published in 1916.

21. Francis Carco was a poet, novelist, dramatist, and art critic who memorialized Parisian bohemia of the early decades of the twentieth century.

22. *Shoulder Arms*, 1918. Soupault himself would later devote an entire volume, *Charlot* (1931), to the character of the Tramp, Chaplin's most famous creation.

23. Likely *L'or* (*Sutter's Gold*), published as a novel in 1925 and filmed in Hollywood in 1936 with a Cendrars screenplay credit.

24. The French *copain* comprises various English terms—buddy, mate, chum, comrade.

25. From "Le tombeau d'Edgar Poe," Stéphane Mallarmé.

26. Gautier famously wore a red vest at the tumultuous premiere of Victor Hugo's *Hernani*, which originated the genre of Romantic drama in France.

27. Tr.: Wallace Fowlie, who, in *Rimbaud: Complete Works, Selected Letters* (University of Chicago: 1966), p. 311, attributes this passage to Rimbaud's May 15, 1871, letter to Paul Demeny.

28. *Paris Spleen*, tr. Louise Varèse (New York: New Directions, 1970), pp. ix-x.

29. Elisabeth Rachel Félix, French theatrical actress, 1821–1858.

30. *Paris Spleen*, p. x.

31. *Paris Spleen*, p. ix.

32. "Anywhere Out of the World," *Paris Spleen,* p. 99.

33. Although Soupault transcribes as "*grandes courses*," most editions provide "*grandes courbes*," i.e., "curves."

34. *Paris Spleen*, p. 49.

35. This painting (*The Last of the 51st Rank*) was juxtaposed at the 1893 Salon des Artistes Indépendants with another Rousseau composition titled *La liberté* that was accompanied by the quoted inscription, according to RIHA Journal 0048, 24 July 2012, Special Issue, "New Directions in New-Impressionism."

Philippe Soupault (1897-1990) served in the French army during WWI and subsequently joined the Dada movement. In 1919, he collaborated with André Breton on the automatic text *Les champs magnétiques*, launching the Surrealist Movement. In the years that followed, he wrote novels and journalism, directed Radio Tunis in Tunisia, and worked for UNESCO.

Poet **Alan Bernheimer**'s most recent collection is *The Spoonlight Institute*, published by Adventures in Poetry in 2009. He has lived in the Bay Area since the late 1970s, where he was active in Poets Theater and produced a radio program, "In the American Tree," of new writing by poets. He has translated works by Robert Desnos and Valery Larbaud.